FEATS AND WISDOM OF THE ANCIENTS

Cover: Seen at sunset not long after the summer solstice, the enigmatic ruins of Stonehenge testify to the surprising astronomical knowledge and building skills of the ancients.

FEATS AND WISDOM
OF THE ANCIENTS

By the Editors of Time-Life Books

TIME-LIFE BOOKS, ALEXANDRIA, VIRGINIA

CONTENTS

SAGES

S mug in the certainty that we stand in the vanguard of history's forward march, modern humans tend to regard the past as little more than a backdrop for current achievements. Progress, we think, has been a steady, linear advance, leading inexorably from superstition to enlightenment, from primitivism to sophistication, from ignorance to knowledge.

This comfortable assumption is being challenged, however, as archaeologists, historians, and other scholars point out evidence hinting that humankind's progress has been less a lockstep march than a lurching dance, with steps forward and steps back, with bursts of genius ahead of its time and lost knowledge that even now rests unretrieved—or is gone forever. The destruction of the Alexandria Library, the greatest repository of learning in the ancient world, resulted in the permanent loss of untold numbers of monumental works of literature and science.

Fortunately, other advances of the ancients have been recorded on substances hardier than papyrus, giving us a glimmer of the level of sophistication of so-called primitive humans. So small a thing as the clay pot shown above, for instance, suggests to some scholars that ancient Andean Indians, long thought to have lacked a written language, may have had one after all (page 13). We now know that the roots of democracy may have been planted in Sumer as early as 3000 BC. And there is evidence that the first notation by humans—perhaps even an attempt at astronomy or arithmetic—may date back to 35,000 BC.

How much more did our ancestors know? In our own ignorance, we are just beginning to learn the answer.

1

The Tragedy of Alexandria

It was the sum and apex of ancient knowledge, a matchless monument to the human intellect—and, ultimately, the victim of human bigotry and ignorance. The Alexandria Library held uncounted masterpieces of science and literature, the sole copies of works now vanished from the earth.

The institution was founded near the end of the fourth century BC by Ptolemy I, a Macedonian Greek general under Alexander the Great, and, rumor had it, Alexander's illegitimate half brother. Following Alexander's death in the year 323 BC, it fell to Ptolemy to rule Egypt, including the cosmopolitan port city to which Alexander had given his name.

A shrewd and farsighted king whose dynasty would hold sway in Egypt for almost 300 years, Ptolemy in his youth had probably studied with Alexander under the great philosopher Aristotle, and he had an appreciation of learning that he would pass down to most of his successors. He wanted to crown his kingdom with a center of knowledge and research, attracting the civilized world's finest philosophers, scientists, poets, and scholars and freeing them from financial worries so that they could devote their complete attention to research, writing, and lecturing.

The library itself was the jewel of Ptolemy's grand scheme, though not the whole of the plan. It was attached to a university and a research institute—called the Museum, after the Muses, the nine Greek goddesses of the arts and sciences. An estimated 14,000 students at the Museum studied physics, engineering, astronomy, medicine, mathematics, geography, biology, philosophy, and literature under the world's best teachers. Everything that these revered pedagogues required was provided for them: comfortable apartments, a dining hall, a chemical laboratory, an observatory, an anatomical theater for observing operations and dissections, and a zoological and botanical garden.

Details of the library's physical layout are uncertain, but scholars do know that it was divided into two parts. The main facility, known as the Royal Library, was evidently a building next to the Museum. Some distance away in the city's old Egyptian quarter was a second library, housed in the Serapeum, the pagan Temple of Serapis. Both buildings were repositories for books handwritten on papyrus scrolls.

To assemble a book collection superior to all others, the Ptolemys and their librarians spared no effort. Legions of learned men, assistants, and highly trained slaves ceaselessly organized, classified, and copied huge stacks of rolls that seemed always to be increasing. At times the library's methods of obtaining the best versions of coveted works were not overscrupulous. While many rolls were purchased fairly by the Ptolemys' minions, ships docking at Alexandria had to surrender any works on board to the library—after which cheap copies would be returned to their hapless owners.

Obviously, since copyists sometimes made mistakes, originals or authenticated versions of valued works were considered far more desirable. Ptolemy III is supposed to have "borrowed" from the city of Athens the official rolls containing the works of the foremost Greek tragedians, Aeschylus, Sophocles, and Euripides. He left a large deposit as security. But instead of returning the scrolls, the king simply forfeited the deposit, and he sent back copies to the furious Athenians.

Such zeal paid off. By the time that Julius Caesar conquered Egypt in the middle of the first century BC, the collection of volumes at the Royal Library numbered between 300,000 and 500,000, with perhaps 50,000 more in the Serapeum. Even though it sometimes took many scrolls to make up a complete book, the number of works at the Alexandria Library would compare respectably to that of a good college library today. But modern books are printed in thousands of copies and cataloged by machines. In an era when books were written, copied, and cataloged by hand, half a million volumes was a truly stupendous number. In fact, in 1450, before the invention of movable type, all of Europe possessed only a tenth as many books as had been housed in the Alexandria Library.

No one is sure precisely what was there. The Ptolemys' mission—never wholly fulfilled—was to acquire an edition of every work by every Greek author. In addition, library translators rendered into Greek important works from India, Persia, and Africa, and the Hebrew scriptures. The literary wealth alone must have been staggering, and the scientific and philosophical holdings equally vast. The shelves of dramatic poets, for example, probably contained not just the 44 greatest Greek plays extant today but all 123 tragedies of Sophocles, along with most or all of the 90 tragedies of Aeschylus, the 92 of Euripides, and the 54 comedies of Aristophanes. Furthermore, thanks to the Ptolemys' support, Alexandria fostered much of the intellectual inquiry of its day, and it generated an enormous amount of scientific research and writing. Even after Egypt became part of the Roman Empire in 30 BC, the library continued as the scientific capital of the world.

But if the library's growth is one of the most inspiring stories in humankind's intellectual journey, its ending was that trek's most tragic event.

Little more is known about the library's destruction beyond the basic facts. Its first brush with disaster came in 48 BC during Julius Caesar's conquest of Egypt. Several thousand volumes were accidentally consumed in a fire started by Caesar's troops at the harbor. Luckily for Alexandria, the famous general Mark Antony later made up at least part of the loss by requisitioning 200,000 volumes of the Pergamon Library in Asia Minor. The love-besotted Roman soldier presented them as a gift to Egypt's brilliant queen Cleopatra.

Unfortunately, there was no Mark Antony to save the library from the savage attack that all but destroyed it. In AD 391, the Christian emperor Theodosius I, at the urging of Alexandria's fanatical bishop Theophilos, ordered the Temple ⟡

The Alexandria Library was founded by Ptolemy I *(far left)* and was the repository of works by ancient Greece's greatest intellectuals, among them, from left to right, tragedians Sophocles, Aeschylus, and Euripides, and philosopher Aristotle.

of Serapis to be destroyed. A mob attacked the Serapeum and burned most of its priceless contents. It appears likely that Christians also pillaged the larger Royal Library, although it is not known exactly how much of that repository perished at their hands.

In any case, whatever was left of the Alexandria Library was finished off after about AD 640 when Arab legions swept through Egypt on their mission to conquer the world for Islam. It is reported that the Arab military governor, baffled by the dusty scrolls in the library, asked Mecca what to do with them. Burn them, he was told, for "either the manuscripts contain what is in the Koran, in which case we do not have to read them, or they contain what is contrary to the Koran, in which case we must not read them." The books were used as fuel for Alexandria's 4,000 public baths. There were evidently enough left to heat bath water for several months. The last of the treasures of antiquity blazed brightly one last time and were gone. Enlightened Arab scholars later recovered from other sources some important works of Greek science and philosophy, such as the writings of Aristotle and Archimedes. But it would be centuries before humankind could begin to reconstruct the knowledge that was lost at Alexandria. □

Alexandrian Scholars

Here are only a handful of the great thinkers who were associated with the Alexandria Library during its 600-year history:

• Euclid (fourth century BC) was a Greek mathematician whose *Elements of Geometry*, used as a textbook for more than 2,000 years, is one of the most important books in Western thought and education.

• Apollonius of Perga (third century BC) was a mathematician who first demonstrated elliptic, parabolic, and hyperbolic curves. The great sixteenth-century German astronomer Johannes Kepler, who first described the elliptical orbits of planets, owed his discovery to Apollonius.

• Archimedes of Syracuse (third century BC) was a mathematician, physicist, engineer, and inventor. A Renaissance-style genius, he is credited with having invented the Archimedes screw, a kind of pump, and other mechanical devices. He is perhaps most famous for discovering his First Principle—that a solid body immersed in liquid is buoyed up by a force equal to the weight of the liquid displaced— while taking a bath.

• Aristarchus of Samos (third century BC) was an astronomer who, 1,700 years before Copernicus, discovered that the earth moves around the sun. Aristarchus also argued that day and night are the result of the earth turning on its axis.

• Herophilus of Thrace (around 300 BC) is remembered as "the father of scientific anatomy." He was the first scientist to prove that the brain, not the heart, was the organ of thought.

• Eratosthenes (third century BC) was an all-around genius. A director of the library, a mathematician, astronomer, geographer, and philosopher, he also wrote poetry and was a literary and theater critic. Using only reasoning and his powers of observation, he accurately calculated the sizes of the earth, sun, and moon.

• Hipparchus of Nicea (second century BC) was an astronomer who made the first known Western chart of the constellations and estimated the brightness of stars.

• Hero, or Heron, of Alexandria (first century AD) was a mathematician and inventor. One of his writings described a steam engine. Probably because unlimited slave power made it unnecessary, this invention was not developed. Hero is also said to have written the first book on robots. □

Strings That Bound an Empire

When Spanish conquistadores chanced upon the vast Incan empire in the 1500s, they found people who were, in many respects, at least as advanced as themselves—with the notable difference that the Inca had no conventional form of writing. What the emperor and his subjects used instead was the *quipu*, a bundle of elaborately knotted strings with which they recorded virtually every important aspect of their civilization. The system worked "with such accuracy that not so much as a pair of sandals would be missing" from the empire's gross store of goods, marveled Spaniard Pedro de Cieza de León in an account he wrote of his 1549 travels in the New World.

A quipu—the Quechuan word for "knot"—typically consisted of a main cord from which were hung about a hundred strings of various colors and lengths. Often more strings were hung from the primary strings, making for a bundle of as many as several thousand strings.

The position and number of knots on a string had precise meaning. A single knot at the top signified 1,000, a knot at the next level was 100, and a knot at the end of the string was the number 1. A cluster of four knots, depending on their location, represented 4,000, 400, 40, or 4. Read from right to left, the strings provided a formidable database. Colors may have added further meaning—white for peace, yellow for gold or corn, red for blood or war.

The quipu was integral to Incan life. While the emperor referred to it for strategic matters, such as the size of his army, an Incan family used its quipu to keep a precise accounting of property such as gold, silver, clothing, corn, or llamas. Upper-class males were expected to learn how to read a quipu, and each district of the empire employed a few expert *quipucamayocs*, or knot keepers, to keep quipus on matters such as tax revenues and census data.

But while quipus functioned primarily as tallies, they also had verbal components. Cieza de León and others reported that they were used as aids in tracking and recounting the oral history of the Inca. Although the chroniclers were vague as to exactly how the system worked, they indicated that the quipus were used to call to mind songs, legends, laws, and traditions. And it was by quipu that the Incan king received the fatal news that the Spanish had landed on his shores.

Although they extended and perfected the art, the Inca were not the first to use knotted strings for recordkeeping. There is evidence that an earlier Andean people may have used quipus for tallying around the year 700. Moreover, the *I Ching*—an ancient Chinese book of philosophy and divination—indicates that, probably in the first millennium BC, the Chinese "were governed by means of the system of knotted strings." Even today, laborers in the Ryukyu Islands between Japan and Taiwan knot ropes to record workdays, and Bolivian and Peruvian Indians—descendants of the Inca—use a device they call a *chimpu* to keep track of livestock. □

Caption (top left):

Excavated in Turkey in 1961, this kitchen cutlery was used by people of the New Stone Age, perhaps as long ago as the seventh millennium BC.

Spoons for Escargots

While Europeans ate with their fingers and their knives until the sixteenth century, a number of ancient civilizations had table manners that were more refined.

The Greeks and Romans, for example, crafted spoons from bronze and sometimes from silver; the Romans had forks as well. But it was the Egyptians, as early as 3000 BC, who fashioned the most ornate and intricate cutlery. Some of the Egyptian spoons even had spiked handles—used for extracting snails from their shells. □

Evolutionary Thinking

In the nineteenth century, Charles Darwin stunned the world with his theory of evolution—the idea that all forms of life evolved through a natural selection process that favored the survival of the fittest. The range and depth of evidence Darwin used to support his theory were unprecedented, but the basic idea was not, in fact, altogether new. Some 1,800 years earlier, the Roman philosopher-poet Lucretius seemed to anticipate Darwin in arguing that the earth had once produced numerous species of creatures that were unable to secure food, protect themselves, or reproduce properly. Because they lacked these essential survival skills, the philosopher opined, the creatures became extinct. □

Calendar of Stone

Ancient Mayan astronomers put the exact length of the year at 365.2420 days. The modern Gregorian calendar puts it at 365.2425 days. Since the actual duration of a year is precisely 365.2422 days, the old Mexican Indian calendar was more accurate than the one commonly used today.

The complex Mayan calendar was not, however, a very portable one. A stela (*left*) from the Mayan ruins at Copan in Honduras displays calendric symbols adding up to one day—July 26, 736, by Gregorian reckoning. □

A Lima Bean Language?

Workers excavating a Mochica Indian grave site in Peru during the mid-1930s may have been disappointed at one of their finds: A small llama-hide pouch turned out to contain nothing more valuable than dried lima beans. But for a Peruvian archaeologist by the name of Rafael Larco Hoyle, the discovery helped confirm a long-held theory: The Mochica—Andean Indians who flourished from about AD 100 to 800 and were eventually absorbed by the Incan empire—communicated through marks on *pallares,* a kind of lima bean.

Decorated with lines, dots, and colors, lima beans appear frequently in Mochica art. So, too, do runners—many pieces of Mochica pottery often depict men dashing across a desert carrying pouches similar to the one found in the grave. Often the two themes are combined; much of the pottery shows lima beans with men's faces, arms, and legs.

While it was widely assumed that the Mochica had no form of writing, Larco Hoyle maintained the lima bean designs were actually crude hieroglyphics, and he found similarities between some of the painted beans and the figures drawn by the Maya, who had a script. Larco Hoyle argued that the system of runners, used by the Inca to carry *quipus* from town to town *(below),* was really a Mochica idea. Not all scholars are convinced that the painted lima beans were communication tools. Some think that they may have been recordkeeping devices, like the quipus *(page 11).* Others believe that they were used in divination or gambling, and that the runners carrying bags of beans were merely playing a game. □

Atomic theory began not with Albert Einstein but with the Greek philosopher Democritus, who speculated in the fifth century BC that all matter is composed of irreducible particles "infinite in number and imperceptible because of the minuteness of their size."

Graven in Clay

Perhaps as long as 5,000 years before true writing arose in Sumer, Mesopotamian merchants and overseers may have come up with a useful precursor to it.

According to Middle Eastern scholar Denise Schmandt-Besserat, by the ninth millennium BC people were using small clay tokens in geometric forms in order to represent the commodities that they were buying, selling, or storing. Based on inscriptions on later tablets, Schmandt-Besserat determined that each shape and design had a specific meaning: A round disk with a cross indicated a sheep, a rectangle represented a granary, and a triangle etched with several lines meant metal. Spheres in a variety of sizes stood for different numbers.

Toward the end of the fourth millennium BC, people began placing the tokens in round clay envelopes about the size of tennis balls. While the clay was still soft, it was marked to show precisely what was inside and then sealed. The system was tamperproof, but it was also unwieldy, and over time it gave way to written tablets.

Not every scholar agrees with the idea that the markings on the envelopes led to writing. Some believe that the earliest instance of writing has been lost and that it actually developed simultaneously with—and independently of—the clay spheres. □

BC High

Five thousand years ago, Sumer had high schools not unlike our modern ones, except that they catered almost exclusively to the elite members of society.

The schools were originally founded for the purpose of teaching script to the children of the wealthy, preparing them for careers as governmental or religious scribes. But curricula eventually expanded, and students could learn botany, zoology, mineralogy, geography, mathematics, theology, grammar, linguistics, and even creative writing.

Archaeologists have found Sumerian workbooks, or practice tablets, dating back to 2500 BC. □

MCCLVI + DXLVIII = ?

Hampered by their own unwieldy numerals, the Romans devised a pocket-size calculator to handle simple problems. A crude form of the bead abacus still widely used in the Far East, the Romans' counting board *(below)* was a small metal tablet. It had several long grooves toward the bottom—each reflecting a higher power of ten—and a matching number of short grooves above. Little spheres in the grooves could be moved up or down to add or subtract. Some of the devices had a few grooves to the right for fractions. □

Starting from Scratch

The concept of zero is crucial to technology, computation, and advanced mathematics. But who pioneered this vital nothing? Several ancient peoples independently evolved the notion of nullity, among them the Babylonians, Chinese, Maya, and Indians.

The zero's story begins with a blank: The Babylonians, perhaps as early as the first millennium BC, and the Chinese, around the fourth century BC, left an empty space to denote the absence of a number. Around 300 BC, the Babylonians filled in the blank with a symbol that suggests a pair of wedges, one atop the other, but that appeared only in astronomical texts, never at the end of a number, and was not used in computation.

The Chinese were evidently able to make sophisticated calculations using only a blank. Their first recorded use of an "oh" shape to indicate zero may have been as late as AD 1247. An excerpt from a 1247 manuscript *(upper right)* shows a Chinese numerical sequence that includes zero in its current form. However, some Indochinese inscriptions from the seventh century bear the modern 0.

More than 1,500 years before the Spanish conquest, the Maya were designing a zero that would ultimately assume a host of shapes and meanings. At times a simple shell, the zero was drawn differently to denote the first day of each month. It was also personified as the god of death, a figure whose hand gripped his lower jaw as if to tear it off—a technique used in human sacrifice. Pictured thus, zero stood for completion. But like the Babylonians, the Maya used zero chiefly to monitor the heavens, not for earthly applications.

In India, the zero first appeared around 200 BC in a Hindu manuscript as a cluster of dots called a *sunya,* or "blank." Over centuries, Hindu mathematicians developed zero's properties, finally giving the symbol its modern form. In the ninth century, the Arabs discovered the Hindu number system and translated *sunya* to *sifr,* which, as the system spread across Europe, was Latinized to *cifra,* or "cipher," and *zepharum,* or "zero." □

An Ancient Bestseller

The *T'ung Shu*—or *Book of Myriad Things*—is almost certainly the world's oldest continuously published book.

Now called an almanac, it started as China's imperial astronomical calendar more than 4,000 years ago, reputedly under the aegis of the emperor Yao—who, according to tradition, reigned from 2357 to 2255 BC. By the time it was available in printed form in the ninth century AD, the calendar had taken on the characteristics of agricultural aid and farmer's almanac.

Over the years, the almanac's contributors have included wise men of the Buddhist, Muslim, Taoist, and Christian faiths. And the book has grown from specialized beginnings to encompass fortune-telling, divination, earth magic, herbal medicine, palmistry, charms, moral codes, dictionaries, predictions, legends, lucky and unlucky days, numerology, and even telegram and telex charts.

Still influential, the almanac continues to sell more than one million copies every year. □

3.14159265

Mathematics' Long March

From decimal fractions to higher numerical equations, the ancient Chinese made significant contributions to the advancement of mathematics.

The development of the decimal system has been traced back to the China of 1300 BC. (The Babylonians may have had a similar system even earlier, but their method used a base of sixty rather than ten.) Both the Chinese and the Babylonians also used negative numbers. Curiously, the Chinese wrote positive numbers in red, negative numbers in black—the reverse of today's Western accounting conventions.

By the third century AD, Chinese mathematicians could compute the approximate value of pi, and by the fifth century, they calculated pi to ten decimal places—a feat unmatched in the West until the sixteenth century. □

"You can have a lord, you can have a king, / But the man to fear is the tax collector!" This Sumerian proverb, from a tablet inscribed around 1800 BC and first translated in 1934, seems remarkably timely.

Gilgamesh Lobbies Congress

Greece may not have been the cradle of democracy after all. Government by the people seems to have blossomed first in ancient Sumer, the desert land lying between the Tigris and the Euphrates rivers in what is now southern Iraq.

What may have been the world's first bicameral congress convened around 3000 BC, almost 2,500 years before the golden age of Athens. According to the great Sumerian epic poem *The Tale of Gilgamesh* (a portion of the saga is on the tablet shown below), the rising and powerful Sumerian city-state Erech was being threatened by a neighbor, Kish, which feared Erech's growing might and was poised to attack its rival. The warrior-king Gilgamesh, Erech's bold ruler, met with what the poem calls "the convened assembly of the elders of his city" to ask them to support resistance against Kish. To his frustration, this upper house voted instead to buy peace by submitting. Undeterred, the king demanded a vote from a lower house made up of men who could bear arms. The hawks won the day.

Nothing more is known about this congress. There are no records from the age of Gilgamesh—writing had barely been invented then —and the tablets that provide this tantalizing glimpse of representative democracy in the ancient Near East were probably written more than a thousand years later. □

Mysterious Marks

When Harvard archaeologist Alexander Marshack slipped the 32,000-year-old fragment of carved reindeer bone *(above)* under his microscope one day in 1965, he felt he had caught a glimpse into the mind of Cro-Magnon man. Under the lens, a serpentine series of incised markings—long regarded merely as random or decorative doodlings of the sort sometimes found on other Ice Age artifacts—suddenly seemed to Marshack to have been made deliberately, repetitively, and with a variety of tools. The scientist concluded that the bone, a tool fragment excavated in the Dordogne region of France in 1911, contained the earliest known human notation. It appears that human beings—cave dwellers—had achieved a form of written communication thousands of years before history's first true writing appeared.

Theorizing even more broadly, Marshack proposed that the artifact's topic was astronomy: Some Cro-Magnon sky gazer had marked the passage of the seasons by chronicling the phases of the moon in a bone "notebook." Marshack has since detected what he views as lunar calendars on some fifteen other Ice Age objects; still other notations, he believes, may be hunters' tallies of animal kills.

Marshack's calendar theory is not universally accepted; some scientists see no particular meaning to the bone markings, while others suggest interpretations that differ from Marshack's. In the latter category is Jean de Heinzelin, a geologist-archaeologist whose explanation of the artifact is no less startling than Marshack's: De Heinzelin suggests that the object's cryptic dashes and dots may constitute the earliest known arithmetic. The people of the last Ice Age, he proposes, had a number system based on ten and were familiar with prime numbers. □

No Stones in the Sky

In the fifth century BC, the Greek philosopher Diogenes of Apollonia, merely by using his powers of observation and reasoning, concluded that "meteors move in space and frequently fall to earth."

More than two millennia later, this perfectly correct notion was dismissed as nothing more than nonsense by the French chemist Antoine Lavoisier, one of the most noted scientists of the Enlightenment. Stones could not fall to earth, Lavoisier asserted, because there are no stones in the sky. □

No Omens in the Sky

While medieval Europeans regarded a comet's appearance with terror and superstitious awe, Greek philosophers in the fifth century BC knew comets for the phenomena they really are—natural objects that reappear regularly in the heavens. Some experts believe that even before the Greeks, ancient Babylonian astronomers understood the true nature of comets. By the first century AD, the Roman historian Seneca was stating—correctly—that comets have orbits, just as the planets themselves do. □

The Transylvanian Tablets

Archaeologists digging into a prehistoric mound in the Transylvanian town of Tartaria in 1961 were only hoping to shed new light on a previously excavated Rumanian site nearby. What they found was dazzling: three small clay tablets *(pictured here)* with signs that looked like writing. Carbon-14 dating suggested that the tablets might date from around 4000 BC, and thus the find hinted at a startling conclusion: Writing might not have originated in the Mesopotamian civilization of Sumer, as had long been thought, but in the barbarian wilderness of eastern Europe.

The three tablets, found in the mound's lowest stratum, were preserved along with some human bones in what had apparently been a sacrificial pit. They bore pictorial symbols resembling inscriptions on tablets both from Sumer and from the highly advanced Minoan civilization of Crete. But if the carbon dating was correct, the Tartaria tablets, made by a primitive Stone Age farming tribe called the Vinca, predated Sumerian writing by one millennium and Minoan writing by two. This idea seemed far-fetched, and indeed there were major problems with it. If writing began in Stone Age Europe rather than in Bronze Age Sumer, it seemed illogical that it leaped to far-off Sumer a thousand years before it reached the much closer island of Crete. Furthermore, prehistorians had already traced the evolution of writing in Mesopotamia, from its pictographic beginnings to a sophisticated system of cursive script. No such evolution had ever been suggested in eastern Europe.

Some experts propose that the carbon dating for the Tartaria tablets was wrong. Others suggest that the tablets were somehow displaced in the mound and that they might have reflected a later period of Vinca culture, one that followed Sumerian writing by a good many years. There is also a theory that the Tartaria inscriptions are not writing at all but a primitive people's uncomprehending copy of "magical" symbols brought to them on the pots and jars of merchants from the more advanced civilization of the Near East. By the time the Transylvanian farmers were copying these pictographs, this theory holds, the Sumerians had long since abandoned such crude script and gone on to more complex forms of writing. □

Credit for discovering how to measure right triangles usually goes to sixth-century BC philosopher Pythagoras. But the Babylonians came up with the Pythagorean theorem more than a millennium earlier, in about 1800 BC.

INVENTORS

Curiosity and ingenuity may not be unique to the human species, but they are certainly among humanity's hallmarks. The youngest child, like the earliest human being, might observe a pebble rolling down a hill, wonder at its movement, pick it up and examine it, toss it, tinker with it—rolling it down a steeper incline or nudging it across a level plane. From such idle tinkering, some vanished person, nameless now for untold millennia, invented the wheel.

For all of the rich fertility of the human intellect, the progress of invention has followed a ragged course, reaching almost explosive levels during certain eras—as when civilization itself dawned in Sumer around 3000 BC—then abating for thousands of years at a time. Moreover, many an innovation has been swept into oblivion by the turbulent currents of history. It is known now, for instance, that the first steam engine was invented not by Scottish engineer and inventor James Watt in the eighteenth century but by an Alexandrian scholar by the name of Hero in the first century AD. Similarly, although Wilbur and Orville Wright pioneered aviation, the brothers may not have been the first people to understand the basics of aerodynamics. The little working model of a glider that is shown above is not a twentieth-century toy but a 2,100-year-old artifact from an Egyptian tomb *(page 28)*. This artifact has suggested to some people that not only did our ancient ancestors understand flight, but they may even have achieved it.

"The best of the new," in the thought-provoking words of an old Russian proverb, "is often the long forgotten past."

Ancient Electricity?

While excavating ruins of a 2,000-year-old village near Baghdad, Iraq, in 1936, workers discovered a mystifying artifact. It was a small earthenware vase in which was set a soldered sheet-copper tube about one inch wide and four inches long. The bottom of the tube was sealed with a crimped copper disk; an iron rod, seemingly corroded by acid, projected through an asphalt plug at the top.

German archaeologist Wilhelm König, then living in Iraq, examined the object and reached a startling conclusion: If the tube had been filled with an acidic solution, it would have served as a rudimentary electric battery. Such batteries, he speculated, may have been used by ancient artisans to electroplate metals. He pointed out that similar objects had been found at other sites in the region, along with thin copper and iron rods that might have been used to link an array of such batteries.

In 1940, Willard F. M. Gray, an engineer at the General Electric High Voltage Laboratory in Pittsfield, Massachusetts, read of König's theory in an article by German rocket scientist Willy Ley. Using drawings and details supplied by Ley, Gray made a replica of the so-called Baghdad battery. When he filled it with a copper sulfate solution, it generated about half a volt of electricity. In the 1970s, West German Egyptologist Arne Eggebrecht took Gray's experiment further. He built a Baghdad battery and charged it with freshly pressed grape juice, as he theorized the ancients might have done. Then he used current from the battery to electroplate a

Asphalt

Copper tube

8"

Iron rod

Asphalt

A cross-section view of a Baghdad battery replica shows an iron rod, insulated with asphalt, protruding from a sealed copper tube. When the copper tube is filled with an electrolyte, the device produces an electric current.

silver statuette with gold *(left)*.

Eggebrecht was all but certain he had confirmed the development and use of electric batteries some 1,800 years before their modern invention by Alessandro Volta in 1799. Moreover, he held that many supposedly gold artifacts from ancient times are really silver, plated with gold in the same manner as his experimental statuette.

Others are not so sure; doubters have observed that the alleged battery might have held only a scroll or a cosmetic. The fact that a modern replica can be made to generate electricity is interesting, they say, but not conclusive proof that this was the object's purpose. □

Topography on Papyrus

Topographical maps—which graphically show natural and artificial features of a given terrain—came into use in the eighteenth century. But there is one such map that is older by almost 3,000 years.

Known as the Turin Papyrus because it is housed in the Egyptian Museum in Turin, Italy, this chart was drawn up around the year 1150 BC. Without question, it is the oldest geological map in the world, and its concern for topographical detail marks the origin of geological thought. Sixteen inches high and six feet across, the Turin map details a ten-mile stretch of land known as Wadi Hammamat and displays roads, quarries, gold mines, and a few buildings that once stood on the site. One of the roads shown, connecting the Nile

Pink shading on the Turin Papyrus map *(top)* corresponds to the actual tint of mountain rocks *(right)* depicted in the photograph; brown streaks on the mountain at the map's top center represent veins of gold. Arrows point to an ancient road still used today.

and the Red Sea, is still in use.

Unlike modern geological maps, which use sophisticated drafting tools and aerial surveys, the Turin scroll is a freehand drawing. It uses color—pink, brown, black, and white—to distinguish topographical features. The shades correspond to the true hues of the landscape: Pink and brown that tint a mountain on the map closely approximate pinkish granitic

rock at the site, while purplish and dark gray indicate similar shades of earth in a nearby quarry.

This pioneering map is attributed to the ancient draftsman Amennakht, chief scribe during the reign of Egypt's Ramses IV. Amennakht is also said to have mapped the burial site of his pharaoh, tinting the sarcophagus reddish brown to match the color of the stone used to fashion the coffin. □

Ancient Secrets of Precious Metal

Fashioned from alloys of precious metals, these masks from Peru *(above)* and Ecuador *(below)* display the skills of pre-Columbian metalworkers.

For more than three millennia, a burial pit in the southern highlands of Peru hid a golden secret. Clutched in a skeleton's fingers was the earliest evidence of metalworking ever to be unearthed in the New World.

The bones were discovered in 1971 by archaeologists who were excavating an Andean grave site some 3,500 years old. Together with several lapis lazuli beads, the fleshless hand held nine small flakes of finely hammered gold foil. At this same burial site were stone implements—two bowls, three hammers, and a small an-

vil—that seemed to make up a gold-working kit. The find meant that the tradition of metalworking in the Americas was 700 years older than previously supposed.

By the time of the Spanish conquest in the sixteenth century, generations of South American Indian metalsmiths had produced an astonishing trove of gold and silver artifacts—or so the conquistadors thought. But when they melted down the looted treasures, the Spanish were often disappointed. It turned out that Andean artisans, possibly to conserve their supplies of noble metals, had learned the techniques of alloying them with copper and treating the finished works so that their surfaces shone with pure gold. Some of the native metallurgists devised a method of depletion gilding, treating their creations with a corrosive chemical that removed only the copper from the surface, leaving behind a film of pure gold. Other artisans plated the copper objects with a thin coating of precious metal.

Metalsmiths of the Moche culture, who inhabited valleys on the northern coast of Peru from about 100 BC to AD 800, were masters of these two techniques. A cache of Moche treasures recently uncovered near the Ecuadorian border included copper alloys that had been plated with gold or silver. Laboratory examination revealed that the plating was remarkably thin and even, measuring less than two microns in certain places.

Perhaps the most startling achievement of the ancient metalsmiths was their manipulation of platinum, one of the rarest and most precious of ornamental metals. From the first through the third centuries AD, Indians of the Choco region of present-day Colombia mined platinum to make jewelry. They discovered that they could work platinum by grinding it into a powder and mixing it with gold dust. Using charcoal fires intensified with forced air drafts from blowpipes, the artisans melted the gold and used it to coat the platinum particles. While the mixture was still hot, they hammered it out and then repeated the process, eventually producing a malleable form of platinum. This technique, called sintering, would not be mastered by Europeans until the nineteenth century. □

The Durable Pillar of Delhi

In the courtyard of the Ktub Minar Mosque in Delhi, India, stands a six-ton iron pillar more than twenty-three feet high. Raised in the fourth century AD, the smooth, blue-black column has long puzzled those who marvel at its size and wonder why this particular pillar—unlike other, similar iron shafts in the region—remains in almost perfect condition, exhibiting only a faint dusting of rust after standing exposed to the elements for 1,600 years.

Until a few decades ago, many experts held that such a huge piece of metal could not have been formed even in the most advanced European foundries before the nineteenth century. Now, however, most agree that the Delhi pillar was not forged in one piece but fashioned from a number of smaller pieces of hot wrought iron that were hammered together using a now-vanished technique known as forge welding.

According to some metallurgists, this method of manufacture may account for the pillar's resistance to corrosion. Repeated hammering and heating, they say, would have permitted a layer of oxide and slag to come to the surface and form a protective coating. Others, though, contend that the basic composition of the pillar—

which is higher in phosphorus and lower in manganese than is modern iron—accounts for its durability. Still others believe that although the pillar's composition and its means of fabrication may have helped, its rustless condition owes a great deal more to the relatively dry, pollution-free atmosphere of Delhi. □

A pottery bottle with a screw-top cap was discovered in 1985 in a Mayan tomb. Prior to that time, the threaded screw was believed to be solely an Old World innovation.

The Steel of Islam

When Christians set out to wrest the Holy Land from the Muslims in the Middle Ages, they met with steely resistance—Saracen swords so strong and sharp that they could fell a Crusader or bisect a feather floating in midair with almost equal ease. The blades were made of Damascus steel, a high-carbon metal whose unusual properties cannot be duplicated even today; modern metallurgists have attempted in vain to penetrate the lost secrets of its manufacture.

Damascus steel got its name because Europeans first encountered it—much to their sorrow—in Syria, whose premier city was Damascus. In fact, this extraordinary steel was made in India, where it was called *wootz*. Traders sold it in India, Persia, Turkey, and Russia, where it was forged into weaponry and other items. The best blades—including the ones that were used against the Crusaders—are thought to have been produced in Persia. However, the origins of the steel may have predated the Crusades by about 1,300 years. Alexander the Great is believed to have encountered Damascus steel during his conquests sometime in the fourth century BC.

The art of making Damascus steel was lost in the middle of the nineteenth century when firearms became humankind's weapon of choice. Contemporary scientists can only guess at the precise techniques of heating, cooling, and forging that must have gone into

A Fatal Offering

Legend has it that in the first century AD, an obscure craftsman brought a gift to the august Roman emperor Tiberius. The offering was a drinking cup, not noteworthy for its beauty, but extraordinary indeed in its properties. It looked like silver but was much lighter, and when its maker hurled it against a stone floor, it did not break, as silver might have done. Instead, it dented in the manner of bronze. The metalsmith promptly repaired the damage with a small hammer. The emperor was amazed.

The story of the metalworker's gift was recorded some years after Tiberius's death in AD 37 in the writings of the court wit Petronius and the natural historian Pliny. Petronius recounted that it was made of "a kind of glass which could not be broken," and Pliny said it was "a vitreous combination which was flexible and ductile."

What was the strange cup made of? Petronius and Pliny seemed themselves doubtful of claims made for the vessel. Based on their descriptions of it, however, modern experts have speculated that it might have been fashioned from aluminum. Like aluminum, the metal resembled silver but was lighter in weight. It could be worked and shaped. And, when questioned by Tiberius, the craftsman revealed that it was extracted from clay—just as aluminum is.

If the metal truly were aluminum, the ancient metalsmith was centuries ahead of his time. Although its compounds are common, metallic aluminum does not occur in nature and is not known to have been isolated until 1825. Today, aluminum can be obtained only through sophisticated chemical and electrical processes. If Tiberius's supplicant produced the metal 2,000 years ago, he must have used a different method.

Regrettably, the emperor saw to it that the world would never unravel the mystery. The gift-bearer boasted that the secret of the metal was known only to him and the gods; Tiberius, fearing the new metal would render silver and gold valueless, decided to narrow the field. He had the metalworker beheaded, leaving the answer to the cup's riddle to the gods alone. □

its manufacture. The only certainty is that ancient smiths found the secret of infusing steel with a high-carbon content while avoiding the brittleness that usually earmarks high-carbon steel. Their much-prized blades possessed not only strength but a distinctive beauty. During the manufacture of wootz, carbon precipitated out of

A network of wavy lines typical of true Damascus steel can be seen *(closeup, above)* on the blade of this eighteenth-century scimitar from Persia.

the steel in a way that ultimately gave the finished blades intricate surface markings that resembled the patterns of damask textiles.

Hoary records indicate that the most exotic part of the procedure had to do with various methods of quenching the forged blades. An ancient text from Asia Minor, for instance, tells how the blade should be quenched by plunging it into the body of a muscular slave, thereby transferring his strength to the cherished blade. □

Iron Sentinel of Kottenforst

Like the pillar of Delhi *(page 23)*, the so-called Iron Man of Kottenforst is notable for its lack of rust. The Iron Man, which stands on an old imperial hunting ground near Bonn, West Germany, is a squared, solid pillar seven feet long, with about half its length protruding above ground.

Its age and origins are not absolutely certain, but it is probably a boundary marker planted in the early seventeenth century and overlooked by scavengers who later uprooted similar posts to sell as scrap metal. The Iron Man may owe its relatively rust-free state to the hundreds of tourists who touch it every year, perhaps to test the local legend that young women who touch and kiss the pillar will soon find a suitable husband. □

Remains of an Ancient Miner

Long before the first Europeans arrived in Chile, South American Indians mined copper in the bleak Atacama Desert—sometimes with fatal results. In 1899, miners working the still-rich lodes there unearthed the body of an ancient colleague who apparently had died in a cave-in centuries earlier. The corpse had been almost completely mummified by the region's intense, dry heat. Its hands seemed still to grope forward, as if to dig. Even more macabre, over time the body had become impregnated with copper, which had turned it an eerie greenish black. □

A Riddle Cast in Aluminum

The ancient metalsmith who made the strange cup for Tiberius *(page 24)* may have erred in thinking that his metallurgical secret was exclusive to him and the gods. In 1956, archaeologists excavating a third-century-AD grave site in the Chinese province of Jiangsu unearthed about twenty belt ornaments. Some were found to be composed of 85 percent aluminum, alloyed with manganese and copper. The alloy was unusually pure, similar to the type used in modern aircraft.

Some metallurgists have dismissed this oddity as merely the result of a freak accident at an ancient smelter. Others, though, have speculated that the Chinese devised an aluminum refining process, now lost, that did not require the massive energy used in today's refineries. □

Nectar of the Nile

Long before Egypt had its pyramids, it had beer.

In 1989, archaeologists excavating the ancient city of Hierakonpolis on the banks of the Nile River in southern Egypt uncovered a 5,400-year-old brewery where beer apparently was concocted from a mixture of river water, half-baked bread, wheat malt, and date juice. The brewery is the oldest ever to be found. □

An Egyptian brewery worker forces fermented grain through a sieve in this statuette from the twenty-sixth century BC.

The Lights That Fai

Enthusiasts thirsting for anomalies sometimes build a precarious structure of speculation from evidence that is readily explained in other ways. Consider, for example, the curious notion that the ancient Egyptians used electric light.

This fancy centers on wall carvings such as the one that is shown above. The art comes from a subterranean room in the temple of Dendera on the east bank of the Nile north of Luxor. Built in the last century BC and the first century AD, the temple is sacred to the sky goddess Hathor. Beneath it are nine underground chambers, their limestone walls covered with hieroglyphics and reliefs. Archaeologists have yet to fully interpret the walls' messages. No serious scholar, however, subscribes to the anomalists' conclusion: that the large, clublike objects that dominate this scene and several others are light bulbs.

Highlights of this light bulb theory run as follows: The wavy lines inside the "bulbs" are filaments (or, failing that, electric eels that some ancient artist depicted to get across the point that the clubs generated energy). The lines extending from the lotus-shaped bases of the clubs are electrical wires or cables that connect to a rectangular box—a high-voltage generator.

More orthodox interpretations of Dendera's walls require no such wild surmise. The "light bulbs," say most archaeologists, represent the emergence of a serpent form of the god Harsomthus, a son of Hathor, from a lotus. The "electrical wires" are merely the stems of the blossoms. The rectangular "generator" is a pedestal for a minor diety whose upraised arms help support the unwieldy club above it.

Nevertheless, the anomalists contend, there is the matter of the absence of soot: Surely the ancient artist used electric light in creating his subterranean works. If he used torches or oil lamps, there would be soot on the walls.

Again, the more likely explanation is a prosaic one. The artist, not relishing the notion of dirt on his creations, merely wiped the temple walls clean.

In dismissing the light bulb the-ory, the experts add a final point: At the time that the temple was built, Egypt was a province of Rome. It seems highly improbable that the ingenious and acquisitive Romans would have overlooked such a startling phenomenon as electricity, leaving it utterly unrecorded in the annals they bequeathed from their time. □

In AD 577, while enemy armies advanced across the north China plain, the beleaguered women of the Northern Qi kingdom made matches to start the cooking fires. This simple invention did not appear in Europe until 1530.

Soaring through Ancient Skies

As he sorted through dusty, discarded exhibits in the basement of the Cairo Museum of Antiquities one day in 1969, Egyptologist Khalil Messiha noticed something decidedly odd. In a box marked "bird objects," Messiha found a peculiar artifact marked "Special Register No. 6347." The other items in the box were clearly figurines of ordinary birds, but item 6347 looked distinctly nonavian. It had straight wings, a sleek, tapered body, and a vertical tail fin.

Checking museum records, Messiha found that the object, dating from around 200 BC, had been discovered in a tomb near Saqqara, Egypt, in 1898. The antiquarian realized with a shock that he was the first person to see the artifact in more than seven decades. To his twentieth-century eyes, 6347 appeared to be not a bird but an airplane—a 2,100-year-old scale model of a working glider.

Messiha's conclusion provoked an immediate controversy that was only heightened by the findings of a committee of scientists appointed by Egypt's Ministry of Culture to investigate the matter. The committee concluded that the seven-inch-long model, built of light sycamore wood and weighing only 1.11 ounces, seemed to incorporate principles of aircraft design that had taken modern engineers decades of experimentation to dis-

cover and perfect. Moreover, they found, the glider worked. More than two millennia after its construction, it still sailed easily through the air at only the slightest flick of the hand.

Yet, the plane may not have been a glider at all. A jagged spot on the lower tail suggests that a component broke off over the years, leading some investigators of oddities and anomalies to speculate that the model may once have included a propulsion mechanism of some kind.

Theirs is not the majority view. Other researchers suggest the model was intended as a toy or a weathervane and its apparent aerodynamic sophistication is a mere coincidence.

Still, the theorists favoring the possibility of ancient flight point out that the early Egyptians frequently made scale models of things they built—including temples, chariots, and ships—and they maintain that the glider is in fact a miniature of a full-size ancient aircraft.

The Egyptians were not alone, however, in leaving behind tantalizing hints of ancient flight. "To operate a flying machine is a great privilege," a Babylonian text called the *Halkatha* records. "Knowledge of flying is most ancient, a gift of the gods of old for saving lives."

Another Babylonian work, the *Sifr'ala of Chaldea*, contains a detailed—if fragmentary—account of how to construct and fly an airplane. Although the text dates back more than 5,000 years, it contains specific comments on copper and graphite airplane parts and describes the effects of wind resistance on stability.

In 468 BC, the Greek mathematician Archytas took a step beyond theory and modeled a wooden pigeon that actually flew. Hailed as a wonder of the ancient world, the pigeon was powered by an internal mechanism of balanced weights and a mysterious, unknown propulsive agent. Some modern scholars theorize that Archytas used a variation of the jet principles demonstrated centuries later by the Greek scientist Hero. Hero designed a rotating boiler that showed the propulsive effect of a jet of steam. Suspended above a fire, his device spun about as steam shot from its four nozzles.

The early Chinese also had a lively interest in the possibilities of flight. Records inscribed on bamboo tablets some 2,000 years old tell of how the emperor Shun, who reigned between 2258 and 2208 BC, built a flying craft to escape his parents' plot to kill him. Not only did the emperor effect a successful flight, the story goes, but he also tested a primitive parachute, landing unharmed after making his getaway.

Four and a half centuries later, Emperor Cheng Tang is said to have ordered his engineer, Ki-Kung-Shi, to design a "flying chariot," the term still used by the Chinese to describe an airplane. According to legend, the emperor ordered the machine destroyed after a successful flight so that its secrets would not fall into the wrong hands.

In the fourth century AD, the scribe Ko-Hung wrote of a "flying car," fashioned from the wood of a jujube tree, that used "ox leather straps fastened to rotating blades to set the machine in motion." The craft may have been imaginary, but Ko-Hung's description calls to mind a helicopter.

The writings of ancient India are perhaps the richest in tales of aviation. The *Mahabharata*, a work that was probably begun in the fourth century BC, tells of an "aerial chariot, with the sides of iron and clad with wings."

The Hindu *Samara Sutradhara*, an eleventh-century-AD collection of texts dating back to antiquity, holds a wealth of information on flight, treating many aspects of aircraft design and even advising on the proper clothing and diet for pilots. "The aircraft which can go by its own force like a bird is called a Vimana," runs one passage. "The body must be strong and durable and built of light wood, shaped like a bird in flight with wings outstretched. Within it must be placed the mercury engine, with its heating apparatus made of iron underneath."

The text goes on to describe "the energy latent in mercury" at some length; unfortunately, though, it offers little information on how that energy was utilized. Caution, the ancient scholars explained, made them discreet, for "any person not initiated in the art of building machines of flight will cause mischief."

The *Ramayana*, the great Indian epic poem dating from the third century BC, describes a double-deck circular aircraft with portholes and a dome—a configuration reminiscent of twentieth-century flying saucer reports. Fueled by a strange yellowish white liquid, the craft was said to travel at the "speed of wind," attain heights that made the ocean look like "a small pool of water," and stop and hover motionless in the sky.

Although most hints of ancient aviation come from the Middle East or the Far East, the New World is not without some related mysteries. One centers on a gold trinket resting in a bank vault in Bogotá, Colombia. The little bauble is believed to have come from the Sinu culture, a pre-Incan civilization dating between the sixth and ninth centuries AD. About two inches long, the object has wings and an unusual tail arrangement. It is one of a handful of similar pre-Columbian gold trinkets, most clearly depicting birds or insects. Most antiquarians believe the pendant is itself a stylized representation of a bat or some other animal. However, other interpretations abound among theorists who think ◊

A canvas folk painting depicts one of the heavenly chariots that are described in detail in the *Ramayana*, a 2,200-year-old epic poem of India.

Crafted by Quimbaya Indians in pre-conquest Colombia, this gold curio found in a prehistoric grave is one of several South American artifacts that resemble delta-wing jets.

ancient humans mastered flight.

For example, the late biologist Ivan T. Sanderson, one-time head of a group of anomaly enthusiasts called the Society for the Investigation of the Unexplained, examined the pendant in 1969 and rejected outright the idea that it represented an animal. No known animal or insect, he claimed, has the deltoid wings and upright tail shown on the trinket. In addition, Sanderson said, although fish have upright tail fins, they usually have a counterbalancing lower one—an item missing from the pendant. "It is obviously a trinket and an artist's conception of something he had seen," he concluded. "However, it is not a representation of any kind of animal, but it looks just like a very modern, delta-winged, steep-climbing jet fighter." A few pilots and aviation engineers voiced support for Sanderson's extravagant hypothesis, but it drew immediate scorn from most of the scientific world.

Even so, theories of ancient flight persist. Dreams of flying have gripped the imagination since ancient people first gazed up at the birds, admiring their grace, yearning for the freedom implicit in their flight. Hardly a culture has been without its myths and legends of god or human taking wing in some form. But is truth shrouded in such legends? There are scattered tales and artifacts suggesting that perhaps, somewhere, some ancient pioneer gave shape to those imaginings and actually flew. As yet, however, the reality of a long-lost knowledge of aviation remains inseparable from myth, a riddle yet to be unraveled. □

A Fiery Secret Weapon

"It made such a noise in arriving that it seemed like thunder in the sky. It was like a dragon flying through the air."

Thus did one witness describe the wonders of Greek fire, the Byzantine Empire's mysterious flaming weapon that awed all who saw its devastating power. This withering, liquid incendiary (called Greek because Greeks had founded the Byzantine Empire) allowed soldiers and sailors to shower fire on their enemies and blast easily through wooden defense works. Armed with it, the Byzantines turned back fierce Muslim attacks in the seventh and eighth centuries and repulsed later assaults by the Russian Empire.

Greek fire's most remarkable feature was that it burst into flame on contact with water. Pumped through bronze nozzles mounted on the decks of warships, it made a singularly formidable naval weapon.

Like modern military establishments, the Byzantine Empire guarded the secret of its deadly weapon, and even today, chemists can only guess at the formula. Possibly the withering mixture contained petroleum, sulphur, nitrates, lime, and bones, and perhaps even urine. □

Turning Up the Heat

In a manner of speaking, the world's first central heating owed its existence to oysters.

Around 80 BC, an ingenious Roman epicure named Gaius Sergius Orata took an interest in harvesting oysters as a commercial enterprise. In this early attempt at seafood farming, Orata sought a year-round source of warm water, known to promote the growth of the succulent mollusks. He devised a system in which furnaces circulated hot air beneath a series of tanks raised on brick pillars. One thing led to another, and soon Orata had invented the Roman hypocaust system, which was used to heat public baths as well as the private villas of the wealthy.

The hypocaust system entailed the erecting of pillars on a concrete and tile floor. Atop the pillars rested a second, well-insulated floor made of bricks, a layer of clay, and a top layer of stone or marble. One or two furnaces fed by wood or charcoal supplied heat that was funneled through a large pipe or a series of flues into the cavity between the two floors. Furnaces at the public baths were used to heat water at the same time that they warmed the floors. In a subsequent refinement, tile flues were used to distribute heat along the walls *(below)*. □

Harnessing Horsepower

Inventions that seem both small and simple in retrospect can sometimes shape the course of history. A case in point is an efficient horse harness—a device that took more than 1,000 years to make its way to Europe from its origins in China.

Until the eighth century, Europeans had devised nothing better for utilizing horsepower than a throat-and-girth harness—a two-strap affair whose top band went around the horse's throat. Its effect was to start choking the horse as soon as the animal exerted itself. The harness also had serious ramifications for human beings: They had no viable way of using horses to transport goods. This meant, for instance, that ancient Rome, with all its power, had to rely on grain shipped in from Egypt to feed itself. Growing grain in Italy was no problem, but getting it to Rome overland was an insurmountable dilemma.

The only ancient civilization to devise a sensible harness was China, where, in the fourth century BC, some unknown wizard invented the trace harness *(above)*. The load-bearing strap of this contraption went across the horse's breast, allowing the animal to pull and breathe at the same time.

Trace harnesses were introduced to Europe by way of Central Asia when the Avars invaded Hungary in AD 568. Over the next 200 years, they spread across the continent, revolutionizing land transport. □

An Ancient Harvest

In 1834, American inventor Cyrus McCormick developed the first truly efficient mechanical reaping machine, sparking a revolution in agriculture. However, a strikingly similar piece of farming equipment existed in ancient Gaul nearly 2,000 years earlier.

Carved stone reliefs from the first century AD show this early harvester, which resembles an outsize comb mounted on two wheels and is pushed along by a mule or a donkey. Farmers used it to harvest their wheat.

By all accounts, the device was quite efficient. Nevertheless, Gallic farmers abandoned it and reverted to the backbreaking method of harvesting with sickles. Most probably, the early reaper fell prey to the general breakdown of society brought about by the fall of the Roman Empire. □

Rolling On

Far ahead of Westerners in hauling as well as in riding, the Chinese invented the wheelbarrow during the first century BC.

For the first few hundred years after this event, the inventors were coy about spreading the news of their creation, since its military importance was considerable: Early Chinese wheelbarrows could carry hundreds of pounds of supplies each, could transport soldiers, and could be arranged as movable barriers against cavalry charges.

Ancient Chinese wheelbarrows were called such things as wooden ox and gliding horse, conveying some idea of how useful they were: A wheelbarrow could cut in half the number of workers needed for any building project. Unfortunately, the laborsaving bonanza was unknown in Europe until the late twelfth or early thirteenth century. Even today, the world's most versatile and efficient wheelbarrows are found in China. □

Ignoring the Wheel

Beyond question, the wheel is among the most significant technological breakthroughs of all time. By about 1000 BC, it had come into use throughout the Old World, but because wheeled carts did not reach the Americas until the Spanish conquest some 2,500 years later, historians had been assuming that the people of the New World had no independent knowledge of the wheel. In the 1940s, however, they learned otherwise.

In Veracruz, Mexico, at burial sites dating from the first century AD, archaeologists unearthed a number of small clay animal figures, each one possessing a set of completely functional wheels. Some, such as the jaguar shown at right, could also be used as whistles. Other wheeled figures from several different time periods have subsequently been uncovered, showing that the objects were made over a span of several centuries. Their presence in graves indicates that they may have had some spiritual significance.

Why, then, did the people of the New World—who sometimes built elaborate, paved roads to link their cities—fail to make any practical use of the wheel?

Some scholars theorize that the wheel had little workaday utility: Draft animals such as horses or oxen were unknown, making wheeled carts impractical. On the other hand, a lack of draft animals would hardly have stood in the way of the development of wheelbarrows, handcarts, and other such conveyances. And even if carts proved to be unattractive, alternate uses for the device, such as the potter's wheel and spinning wheel, could have been developed. Yet, so far, none has been uncovered. □

Egypt's Edison

The intellectual center of the world at the time, Alexandria, Egypt, in the third century BC produced one of history's great inventors—an individual who might have missed his calling in life had he not been a dutiful son.

The inventor's name was Ctesibius, and his career began when he was apprenticed in the family barbershop. For his father's convenience, the budding inventor devised an adjustable mirror, employing a lead ball in a tube as a counterweight. He found that when the mirror was adjusted, the lead ball compressed the air within the tube and created a loud noise. The discovery intrigued young Ctesibius, who rigged up a cylinder and plunger to carry out further sound experiments. In time, he created the first musical organ. Its design incorporated most of the basic features of modern organs, which produce their distinctive sounds when compressed air is introduced into a set of pipes, each pipe having a different pitch. In order to direct the flow of air, Ctesibius devised the world's first musical keyboard.

Because water pressure was used to force air through its pipes, Ctesibius's instrument was called the hydraulus, or water organ. The heart of the device was a large, inverted funnel immersed in water. Under steady pressure from the water at the funnel's mouth, air was drawn off into the pipes to produce sound. A bellows replenished the supply of air in the funnel. (Later organ makers, building on Ctesibius's work, dispensed with water pressure in favor of powerful bellows.)

Ctesibius's fascination with hydraulics led him to further inventions, including a highly accurate water clock, one of the age's great mechanical marvels. Some 2,300 years after he first tinkered with a barber's mirror, the versatile father of the musical organ is still viewed as a founder of the modern science of hydraulics. □

This Roman clay model of Ctesibius's water organ was found in ancient Carthage.

HEALERS

For many ancient societies, medicine and magic were almost indistinguishable. Thousands of years ago, for example, Egyptian physicians battled not injury and disease, but the demons that invaded their patients' bodies. They invoked Thoth, god of wisdom and sorcery, and chanted an exorcism: "Flow out thou who breakest bones, destroyest the skull, diggest in the bone-marrow and makest the seven holes in the head ill."

But pragmatism existed side by side with magic, and great pioneer physicians, with little guidance but trial and error, observation, and logic, discovered drugs and procedures that successfully combatted the body's ills. These doctors knew nothing of microorganisms, but they concocted salves that healed wounds and prevented infection. Indian surgeons examined human cadavers in order to learn anatomy, so their techniques were especially advanced. They even dared to undertake cataract operations and invented plastic surgery. Hippocrates, the Greek who founded rational medicine in the fifth century BC, built on the contributions of the Egyptians and the Indians.

In the China of the second century BC, divines of the native Taoist religion performed medical experiments of a complexity not to be equaled elsewhere for hundreds of years. Inoculation and endocrinology probably began with them. And a number of useful modern drugs owe their existence to plant-wise peoples who have lived in the South American rain forest for thousands of years.

3

Using copper or bronze implements such as these, early Peruvian surgeons operated on the skulls of hundreds of injured warriors.

Ancient Brain Surgery

One day in the early 1860s, an American diplomat and amateur archaeologist named E. G. Squier was browsing through a private archaeological collection in Cuzco, Peru, when the skull of a pre-Columbian Indian caught his eye. Squier's attention was drawn to a small rectangular hole in the bone: It could, he concluded, only have been cut by a human hand. Squier bought the skull and packed it off to Paul Broca, a prominent French physician and anatomist.

Late Stone Age tombs in France had yielded skulls with similar artificial holes. Anthropologists assumed the holes had been made during religious or magical rituals performed after an individual's death; the operation was called trepanation. But when Broca examined the Peruvian skull, he made a startling discovery. The hole, he announced, could not have been cut after death because an infection had left characteristic pockmarks in the surrounding bone. He estimated that the patient must have survived for at least a week after trepanation for the infection to have developed.

Following Broca's lead, anthropologists took a new look at the Neolithic French finds and discovered that many of these skulls, too, had been trepanned during life and not after death. Extensive evidence of the ancient surgical procedure also turned up in other European countries, as far east as Russia, although the pre-Columbian Peruvians seem to have performed trepanation on a scale that was unequaled at any other time or place. More than a thousand trepanned skulls have been found in Peru, a number greater than in all the other countries of the world combined.

Most of the Peruvian skulls are from adult males, and most bear the marks of terrible blows to the head. Almost certainly, the men were warriors injured in battle by maces or projectiles from slingshots. Surgeons apparently trepanned their skulls not in rituals, but for purely therapeutic reasons, such as removing bone pressing on the brain or relieving swelling. The Peruvians, in short, practiced medicine, not magic.

Not so the earlier Neolithic surgeons, whose motives appear to have been linked more to ritual than to healing. Few of the Eu-ropean skulls show signs of injury, and in France, most of the subjects were women. Why this was so remains a mystery—as does the meaning of some intriguing discs archaeologists have gathered in Neolithic tombs.

Called rondelles, the discs are made of polished, perforated cranial bone. They appear to be amulets or talismans that were worn around the neck to ensure good fortune or ward off evil spirits. Each rondelle was cut from the skull of a dead person but only from an individual who in life had undergone trepanation: The rondelle encompasses an arc of bone taken from the edge of a trepanned hole. What magical or religious power Neolithic peoples believed to suffuse trepanned bone can only be guessed.

Magic and therapy may have merged in some trepanations. Primitive peoples commonly blamed demons for illness. Thus, cutting a hole in the skull must have seemed

36

a logical way to rid the body of a resident devil, especially in diseases such as mental illness that appeared to arise in the head. Over time, though, trepanation's medical uses came to predominate in Europe. By the fifth century BC, Hippocrates and other medical authorities were recommending it as a treatment for head injuries.

Because of their sheer numbers, Peruvian skulls have provided much information about the procedure. For making a hole, surgeons had a choice of four techniques: scraping, boring, cutting, and incising. Each required a special instrument, usually of copper or bronze. Using such implements, Paul Broca tried the procedure on cadavers and found that it took as little as a half-hour—mercifully short for a badly-wounded, comatose warrior, but no doubt endlessly long for a conscious patient with access to no anesthetic except alcohol or hallucinogenic herbs.

Typically, the operation involved making a single hole one to two inches across. However, multiple openings were often made, and some patients returned for repeat surgery. One skull has openings from seven trepannings. Considering the dangers of infection and uncontrolled bleeding, the survival rate was high: About 50 percent of the Peruvian patients survived, judging by the degree to which their skulls had healed.

Ancient European patients could have faced trepanation with a good deal of confidence, for more than 80 percent of them survived—no doubt because, unlike the Peruvian warriors, they went under the knife in good health. But pathologist Arthur C. Aufderheide of the University of Minnesota has noted that a neurosurgeon of 1900 would have been pleased to have his patients pull through as often as even the Peruvians did. Fully 75 percent of a turn-of-the-century brain surgeon's patients were likely to die, usually from infection. Ancient peoples evidently did not have to contend with infectious organisms as virulent as those in the crowded modern world. □

Disease to Cure Disease

In the eleventh century AD, a Taoist hermit living on a mountain in the Chinese province of Sichuan learned that the prime minister, Wang Dan, had sent a desperate summons throughout the empire: Anyone who knew how to prevent or cure smallpox was to come to him. His eldest son had just died of the disease, and he feared the rest of his family might succumb.

Answering the summons, the old hermit journeyed to the imperial capital, bringing with her a number of smallpox scabs. She placed them on bits of cotton that she inserted into her patients' noses—and thereby demonstrated the esoteric Taoist practice of inoculation.

The story of the hermit, which appeared in a mid-sixteenth century text on China's imperial medical tradition, may blend measures of myth and reality. Other tellings of the tale describe the hermit as either a monk or a nun. Even so, inoculation—the controlled introduction of a virus to stimulate the body's manufacture of protective antibodies—is without doubt a Chinese innovation, and it may have sprung from the work of Taoist alchemists. Unlike their Western counterparts, these early scientific researchers sought the elixir of eternal youth not in a laboratory, but within their own bodies. Perhaps, in their search for this elusive substance, they stumbled on the technique of inoculation.

By the late sixteenth century, Chinese physicians knew of a relatively safe version of the practice. The worst cases of smallpox are caused by *Variola major;* a second smallpox virus, *Variola minor,* is not so lethal. Physicians distinguished between the symptoms of the two strains and used scabs from people infected with the milder type for inoculation. And, instead of taking scabs produced by a full-blown case of smallpox, they used scabs from people who had recently been inoculated. They thereby obtained a weakened virus—one incapable of causing the illness but still strong enough to trigger antibody formation.

Another technique for ensuring a safe supply of viruses involved having the physician wrap the scabs in paper, seal them in a tightly corked bottle, and carry them around with him for a month. During that time, about 80 percent of the hardy viruses would die from the doctor's body heat, rendering the scabs safer for use. □

China's Early Endocrinology

Endocrinology, the medical specialty dealing with hormone-producing glands, enjoyed a landmark year in 1890. That was when Western doctors came up with a revolutionary treatment for thyroid hormone deficiency. The science took another giant step in 1927, when two researchers announced that they had discovered a rich supply of sex hormones in the urine of pregnant women.

But such breakthroughs in the West were old news in China. Some 2,000 years earlier, Chinese physicians routinely cured goiter, a condition in which the thyroid gland fails to manufacture enough of the hormone thyroxine, essential for the body's metabolism. The cause of goiter is a lack of iodine, and the Chinese treatment was simple: Their cure involved the use of seaweed, a rich source of iodine. By the fifth century they had devised ways to concentrate the active ingredient into pills and a wine-based tincture. The Chinese observed that goiter was common in some mountainous areas and surmised, correctly, that the soil and water must somehow be deficient.

A Chinese pharmacopoeia of the early seventh century reported a still more sophisticated treatment called organotherapy. Thyroid glands from sheep were chopped and combined with fruit in pill form. A cruder variation required patients to be dosed with raw glands. Organotherapy supplied both iodine, which the body concentrates in the thyroid gland, and thyroxine itself—a special boon in cases where disease had diminished or destroyed the gland's ability to produce the hormone.

As remarkable as this therapeutic achievement was, it was matched by another—the treatment of sexual disorders with sex and pituitary hormones extracted from urine. At least as early as 125 BC, Chinese alchemists are known to have produced from concentrated urine a hard, white crystalline substance called autumn mineral. These pioneer endocrinologists could alter the effect of the autumn mineral by varying the proportions of male and female urine. Impotence, menstrual disorders, even cases of hermaphroditism and sex reversals were treated with urine extracts.

Their effectiveness was probably unpredictable, however, owing to the uneven quality of the medicine. The alchemists developed a variety of techniques for producing autumn mineral. All were major undertakings that required many participants, since 150 gallons of urine yielded a mere two or three ounces of autumn mineral.

But modern research has revealed that only one of the methods would have yielded a hormone-rich substance. In that process, evaporation of the urine left a powdered residue containing hormones and many impurities. Heating the powder in a closed vessel vaporized the hormones—which then condensed on the cooler surface of the vessel's lid. □

The Healing Power of Honey

An Egyptian papyrus of medical lore dating back to 3,600 years ago lists close to a thousand remedies—and in more than half of them honey is an important ingredient. It was particularly valued in salves, usually in combination with a vegetable or animal fat.

To the chagrin of some modern skeptics, experiments have shown that honey deserved the confidence that Egyptian apothecaries placed in it—a confidence shared by practitioners of folk medicine in many cultures down to the present day. It can soothe a wound and prevent a bandage from sticking. But beyond such mundane virtues, honey has a peculiar and complex chemistry that actively combats infection and speeds healing.

Honey is a potent killer of harmful bacteria. It has an enzyme from bees' laryngeal glands that combines with glucose and oxygen to form the disinfectant hydrogen peroxide and an antibiotic called gluconolactone. Honey is also hypertonic—it readily absorbs water—thus it can keep a wound dry and draw off fluid bacteria need to live.

Moreover, honey has been shown to promote the growth of healthy tissue in some instances. In 1983, for example, Israeli physicians reported on an experiment in which skin wounds on one group of mice were simply cleaned with a saline solution, while wounds on a second group were salved with ordi-

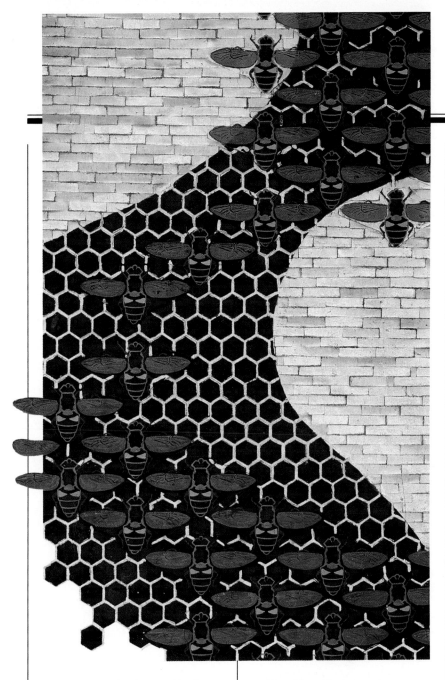

Building New Noses

No feat of ancient medicine outshines what Hindu plastic surgeons accomplished for patients disfigured by mutilation or accident. Among other achievements, these physicians, practicing as long as 2,600 years ago, invented a method of rebuilding noses that is still used in the twentieth century.

There was no lack of patients for reconstructive surgery in ancient India. In addition to missing noses, ripped ears were a major problem. It was customary for everyone, male and female alike, to have pierced ears, and the sheer weight of the large earrings commonly worn could tear the earlobe, as could a vicious yank on an earring during a fight.

Earlobe reconstruction involved surgically lifting a flap of skin from the patient's cheek. The flap was then pulled backward and sutured to the ear to form a new lobe. The *Sushruta Samhita*, the Hindu surgical compendium, advised that after the operation, the patient "should be careful not to disturb the bandage and avoid physical exercise, over-eating, sexual intercourse, exposure to, or basking in the glare of fire, fatiguing talk, and sleep by day." When downy hair began to grow on the new lobe, the surgeon knew that the graft had taken nicely and could soon sport an earring.

Noses were a more complex matter. Amputation was a common punishment for theft, adultery, and any number of far more trivial acts. No body part was sacrosanct, but a person whose nose was ⟡

nary commercial honey. The honey-treated mice grew new skin at double the rate of the first group.

More recently, Nigerian physician S. E. E. Efem tried honey on fifty-nine patients suffering from horrible skin ulcers that had defied conventional treatment for as long as two years. In every case but one, he reported, honey worked where all else had failed. Within a week, swelling and infection subsided,

and healthy skin began to grow.

Since it can kill bacteria, honey defies decay. In the ruins of the ancient town of Paestum in Italy, archaeologists have unearthed some honey, still golden and sticky after 2,500 years in a tomb, where it was left as an offering. The honey had been preserved by its own purity, the same quality Egyptians of long ago found so effective against pain and disease. □

amputated looked hideous and suffered intense humiliation. To the ancient Indians, the nose symbolized one's reputation, so its loss meant a loss of face, literally and figuratively. No longer deserving respect, a noseless person became a social outcast.

The first beneficiary of nose restoration was, according to Indian tradition, a certain Lady Surpunakha, whose nose was amputated on the orders of a prince in 1500 BC. Taking pity on her, the king instructed his physicians to rebuild the lady's nose.

One reconstructive technique described in the *Sushruta Samhita* had the physician use skin from the cheek as the stuff of a new nose. A second version favored skin from the middle of the forehead, but otherwise the procedure was the same. Using a vine leaf the size of the severed nose as a template, the surgeon cut a flap of

skin with a narrow stem-shaped end called a pedicle, which remained attached to the face. He made shallow cuts in the flap to shape the tissue, then rotated it to keep the skin side facing outward, pulled it over the nasal area, and stitched it in place.

To create a functional organ, two little pipes—probably made of bamboo or clay—were inserted at the lower end of the new nose to make breathing easy and help mold a pair of nostrils. The cotton bandage placed over the area was

sprinkled with sesame oil or clarified butter, which helped shield the surgical wound from germs.

Even if the new nose was imperfect it nevertheless restored a patient's reputation and place in society. The rewards of rhinoplasty thus more than repaid patients for the pain they had to endure. □

From Ancient Lore to Mainstream Medicine

At least 3,500 years ago, Egyptian and Sumerian apothecaries whipped up medications containing parts of the willow tree. The Greeks and Romans relied on extracts of willow for earaches, gout, corns, inflammations, and eye infections, and American Indians brewed a medicinal tea from willow bark. Colds, asthma, and what Elizabethan botanist John Gerard described as "the spitting of

Bloud"—probably from pneumonia—called for decoctions of willow bark and leaves.

It was not until the nineteenth century that chemists discovered the old remedy's active ingredient—a bitter-tasting compound dubbed salicin after the willow's Latin name, *Salix*. Once the tree's secret was out, scientific tinkerers went to work on the compound, hoping to improve on nature and

produce a version without such unpleasant side-effects as nausea and stomach cramps. One of their laboratory creations was aspirin, which went on the market in 1899 and was soon hailed as a miracle drug for its power to relieve pain, fever, and inflammation.

Folk medicine brims with plants that, like the willow, ease pain and cure ills. Even peoples regarded as primitive by Westerners steeped in rationalist tradition have highly sophisticated pharmacopoeias, refined from experience that has been passed down orally for untold generations. Ethnobotanist Walter H. Lewis and his wife, Memory Elvin-Lewis, a microbiologist, have studied such groups in their native environments and report that although the Jívaro of the Amazon jungle neither read nor write, they use more than 500 different species of medicinal plants. Troublesome teeth, for instance, are coated with the juice of a mulberry tree and, within ten days, the teeth crumble and fall out painlessly.

Western medicine long ago adopted two Jívaro finds—quinine for malaria, and curare, a paralyzing poison, as a muscle relaxant. The Jívaro are one of a score of Amazonian tribes that use curare to kill or stun prey—and, on occasion, their enemies. The substance is extracted from any of several species of climbing vines, the most potent of which is the moonseed. The active ingredient is an alkaloid that prevents nerve impulses from reaching the muscles. In large doses, it kills. In small doses, it simply eases muscular tension, and surgeons find it invaluable in abdominal surgery. Other drugs, reputed to prevent conception for months, to boost a woman's fertility, or to speed the healing of broken bones, make the Jívaro's plant lore a fascinating and potentially rewarding field of study.

To be sure, modern medicine has not always been open to such preparations. Holy men of ancient India treasured rauwolfia, which they called the moonshine plant, for the relief it gave people suffering from the "moon disease," or insanity. Besides sedating the mentally ill, it was used for snake bite, fever, diarrhea, and dysentery. Holy men chewed its root during meditation, and a mild extract calmed cranky babies.

Rauwolfia was still a popular folk remedy in 1931, when Indian researchers announced that a drug extracted from the plant not only tranquilized disturbed patients but also lowered blood pressure. Yet Western medical scientists continued to ignore the Indian experience. Then, in 1952, rauwolfia was tested in the West. Within two years, the age-old tranquilizer had helped launch a revolution, and drug therapy became standard treatment for mental illness. □

Ancient Salves: Cures and Quackery

The drugs of the ancient world's pharmacopoeia compounded magic and reason in unequal measures. Some substances did benefit patients and are still prescribed today. But the vast majority—they numbered in the thousands and included animal, vegetable, and mineral products in astonishing variety—were sometimes harmful, often ineffectual, and frequently repulsive.

For instance, excrement—from flies, crocodiles, pelicans, even humans—was relied on for complaints ranging from baldness to cataracts. Such substances, repellent to the modern mind, were chosen for a supposed magical potency often reinforced by incantation. Thus an Egyptian physician treating blindness poured liquid extracted from a pig's eye into the patient's ear (in the erroneous belief that a conduit connected ear to eye) as he chanted, "I have brought this which was applied to the seat of yonder and replaces the horrible suffering."

Their peculiarities notwithstanding, some remarkably offensive or seemingly irrational preparations did cure or prevent disease. The Chinese treated eye ailments with bat dung, and patients suffering from at least one condition—night blindness—probably improved. Analysis shows that bat dung has a high level of vitamin A, the active ingredient in an extract of liver prescribed by modern ophthalmologists for night blindness. The ancient Egyptians were even closer to the modern mark than the Chinese in their prescription for the same ailment: "Ox-liver placed over a fire of grain or barley stems and suffused with the vapours they emit, the resulting liquid to be pressed on the eyes."

Infections may have yielded to another Egyptian innovation, a salve of "rotten bread" for wounds. Medical historians speculate that the salve had antibacterial molds comparable to penicillin.

A millipede's chemical defense against predators—a liquid with benzoquinone, an antiseptic—was a favorite ingredient of ancient Greek nostrums for wounds. Because the millipede yields up this substance only when disturbed, Greek physicians first had to alarm the creature. The liquid was then added to the salve. □

Leeching for Health

In ancient times, the principal cause of disease was thought to be an inharmonious balance of the body's essential fluids, or humors. A reasonable treatment, therefore, involved getting rid of excess blood or some other body fluid that seemed to be in oversupply.

Bleeding was sometimes induced with a knife or needle and a suction cup, but another handy and relatively painless implement was the leech, a voracious little bloodsucking invertebrate. A wall painting in the tomb of an Egyptian scribe named Userhat, who died in 1308 BC, appears to show a man hunching on a stool as a practitioner applies leeches to his forehead. What ailed this patient is unknown, but over the years the leech has been employed to treat a long list of maladies.

One of the oldest surviving medical prescriptions dates to the second century BC, when the Greek physician Nicander suggested the use of leeches for venomous bites. Other practitioners prescribed them for epilepsy, headache, pleurisy, insanity, infected wounds, and gout, along with disorders of the eye and ailments of the spleen and other internal organs.

The medicinal leech, a species that inhabits Old World streams and ponds, was the favorite of physicians, who often kept a supply on hand. The inch-long creature has a round mouth housing three cutting plates, each armed with as many as 100 teeth. After piercing its host's skin, the leech feeds steadily for fifteen minutes or so. When its digestive tract has been filled to capacity—it holds as much as two ounces of blood—the leech lets go.

For most patients, from the earliest days to the more recent past, the leech probably did neither harm nor good. Modern surgeons, however, have found that in some respects their ancient counterparts may have had the right idea: Leeches have a decided benefit in delicate procedures such as the reattachment of severed ears or fingers. The blood supply to the reattached member is assured by surgical repair of arteries. But the smaller veins—which carry blood to the heart—must usually be left to heal themselves; until they do, the blood stagnates in the reattached part. When leeches are allowed to remove the blood, pain and swelling are lessened and healing enhanced. The animals also inject an anticoagulant that causes a continued ooze of blood for several hours.

Leeching is, of course, a less than perfect treatment. Many patients are queasy at the thought of it, and a leech harbors a potentially infectious bacterium. Even so, this ancient treatment has so thoroughly proved its benefits that a leech farm in Wales does a lively business supplying tens of thousands of the creatures yearly to surgeons all over the world. □

Living Sutures

The kit of a skillful surgeon in ancient India may literally have been acrawl with a cunning technical aid—a handful of large black ants.

In a medical treatise compiled some 2,000 years ago, the scholar Sushruta indicated that surgeons used ants to suture intestinal wounds. "According to others," he wrote, "large black ants should be applied even to the perforated intestines, . . . and their bodies should be separated from their heads after they had firmly bitten the perforated parts. . . . After that the intestines with the heads of the ants attached to them should be gently pushed back into the cavity and reinstated in their original situation therein."

Modern anthropologists have turned up evidence that peoples in Africa, South America, and Bhutan even today suture wounds with large ants. In South America, soldiers of the species *Eciton burchelli,* an army ant, are used. These creatures have powerful, hooklike mandibles that easily pierce flesh, and dislodging them is a painful and arduous process. Even if the ant is killed in mid-bite, its mandibles maintain their viselike hold. □

The Shining Leg of Capua

More than two millennia ago, a man who must have been something of a dandy stumped about the Roman city of Capua on a handsome and most unusual leg. His own was missing from just below the knee, perhaps lost to a war injury, an accident, or an infection that ended in amputation. Whatever the cause, he declined to make do with a simple peg leg, as people of the time ordinarily did. Instead, the device that he wore had a realistically modeled wood core and a decorative sheath of gleaming bronze.

The Capua leg went to the grave with its owner around 300 BC and remained undiscovered and unnoted until the late nineteenth century. Even then, the leg drew only casual attention—although, as far as anyone knew, no other prosthetic device built in the classical era ever resembled the form, as well as the function, of the bodily member that it replaced. No false foot was found in the grave, and, although iron rods pierced with holes were attached to the top of the bronze sheath, it remains uncertain exactly how the leg was held in place.

Scholars believe that this prosthesis was the work of a craftsman, not a doctor. Physicians of old seem not to have concerned themselves with artificial body parts; they are unmentioned in any surviving classical medical text.

Somehow the Capua leg came to rest at the Museum of the Royal College of Surgeons in London. Around 1910, a facsimile of the leg was made—a fortunate thing, since German bombs destroyed the original in a 1941 air raid. □

Open Wide

Although dental cavities appear to have been relatively rare in Etruscan mouths, loose teeth may have been common. Among many such examples, this skull, found in a tomb dating from the second or third century BC, had been fitted with two thin bands of gold to encircle and steady the teeth along the lower jaw. Using human and oxen teeth, Estruscan dentists also crafted dentures, which were simply riveted to the gold bands.

Clearing the Clouds from Ancient Eyes

Far from being a strictly modern sight-saving miracle, cataract surgery was performed successfully in ancient times.

A cataract is a clouding of the eye's lens that prevents light entering the pupil from reaching the retina at the back of the eyeball. Since the light has to reach this destination in order to create a visual image in the brain, untreated cataracts can eventually cause blindness. Many ancient Indians escaped this unhappy fate, however, because of a Hindu operation now called couching.

Couching is described in *Sushruta Samhita*, a treatise that records Hindu surgical practices prevalent thousands of years ago. The aim of the procedure was to move the clouded lens to a position where it could not obstruct vision. To perform the operation, a surgeon needed a working knowledge of the eye's anatomy, no small measure of boldness, and ambidexterity: The *Sushruta Samhita* advised operating on the left eye with the right hand and on the right with the left.

The surgeon sat on a low stool facing the patient, who was seated on the ground. To prevent the patient from thrashing about in pain, his hands were tied together, and the surgeon's assistant held his head firmly. After inserting a lancet between the iris and the corner of the eye, the surgeon moved the instrument's tip from side to side and upward, listening for a characteristic sound and watching for a drop of liquid emerging from the eye. These signs indicated that the lens was impaled. "If the patient ◊

can see objects," the treatise counsels, "the doctor should draw the lancet out slowly, lay cotton soaked in fat on the wound, and let the patient lie still with bandaged eyes." The fat formed a barrier to bacteria and reduced the risk of infection.

Whether couching was a Hindu invention is impossible to determine. A passage in Hammurabi's Code, which predates the *Sushruta Samhita* by more than one thousand years, hints that Babylonian surgeons were familiar with the operation. Wherever it originated, couching persisted into classical times. But, unlike their Hindu counterparts, Roman surgeons of the first century AD favored penetrating the eye above the iris, rather than beside it, and pushing the lens downward from the pupil. If it resumed its original position when the lancet was withdrawn, the surgeon used the instrument's tip to cut the lens into pieces. The Roman writer Celsus says in *De Me-*dicina that tiny pieces are "more easily stowed away singly and form smaller obstacles to vision."

Around AD 1000, Arabic surgeon and writer Ammar al-Mausili announced that he had made a radical advance in treating cataracts. With a syringelike instrument, he could actually extract the lens instead of couching it and thus prevent any recurrent visual obstruction. It seems, however, that the Romans may have preceded Ammar with this innovation. In 1975, archaeologists found a small cache of ophthalmological instruments at Montbellet, France, once part of Roman Gaul. Along with three small bronze couching needles were two other devices in which a needle was housed in a tiny tube marked with an eye at its tip. The correspondence between Ammar's description of his device and the Montbellet syringe was quite precise, leading medical historians to credit Roman surgeons with being first to use the technique. □

ENGINEERS

The world as it looks today is in many respects a tamed place. Rivers have been dammed, great sections of marshland filled, forests turned into farmland, deserts irrigated. But all this man-wrought transformation began a long time ago—much further back in the past than most people appreciate.

The first alteration of the landscape no doubt occurred tens of thousands of years ago. That exercise of the human will may only have been a mound of earth, scraped together and heaped high to commemorate some momentous event or to venerate a newly fallen chieftain. Or it may have been a pile of stones, raised to honor some fearful but now-forgotten god. Time and wind and rain have scrubbed away such early monuments. But the die had been cast, and although it had yet to be named, engineering had been born. Indeed, go forward through the centuries to the third

millennium BC, and those mounds have become mountain high and stuffed with treasure, the piles of stones have turned into pyramids, and the species responsible has abandoned its caves and crude huts to build entire cities of handmade brick, with paved streets, neat rows of houses, and plumbing.

Tunnels were burrowed, canals dug, roads laid to last as long as empires—much of this thousands of years before the Christian era began. Few challenges seemed too large to ancient engineers, few obstacles too high, so they gave the world a Stonehenge, a Great Pyramid, and, in the Peruvian Andes, stonework so intricate it still inspires awe *(above)*.

Who were these master builders? No one knows for certain; their names went largely unrecorded or were later lost. But much of what they built remains, if only as splendid ruins—and sometimes as splendid mysteries.

Raising the Pyramids

It weighs some 6,500,000 tons, soars 481 feet above the surrounding desert, and covers more than thirteen acres. Around 2600 BC when it was built, it was honeycombed with booby-trapped passages, chambers, and galleries. In fact, the Great Pyramid of Khufu boasts so many impressive statistics that to call it great seems an understatement—all the more so since it was built without benefit of the wheel or beasts of burden or sophisticated tools or equipment.

Mindful of the challenges the builders of the Great Pyramid must have faced, historians, archaeologists, and Egyptologists have served up a multitude of theories over the centuries to explain its construction. Some of those theories demand a greater leap of faith than others.

In the nineteenth century, for instance, there arose the notion of the "pyramid inch," a divinely inspired dimension that supposedly encoded in micro form a wealth of cosmic information. This arcane measure was the brainchild of Scotland's

Charles Piazzi Smyth, a professor of astronomy at the University of Edinburgh. A devout Presbyterian, Smyth had unbridled enthusiasm for the Great Pyramid's possible spiritual implications. Applying his pyramid inch, which amounted to .999 inches, to the pyramid's inner and outer dimensions, Smyth deduced calculations for the earth's density and equatorial diameter and the distance from the earth to the sun. In addition, by equating each pyramid inch with one year, he found interesting chronologies embedded in the architecture. Among them were the dates for the Hebrews' exodus from Egypt, the birth of Jesus, and, by projection, the end of the world. Writing in the 1860s, Smyth put the final cataclysm at 1881.

In the twentieth century came the claim of a French chemist named Joseph Davidovits that the pyramids were not so much built as poured. In 1974, Davidovits pro-

posed that instead of being quarried and hauled, the stones used to build the pyramids were cast as needed on the spot, employing a process similar to the one used today to make Portland cement. According to Davidovits, crushed limestone was mixed with a special "geopolymeric" binder to create a fluid, epoxylike substance. This mixture was then poured into wooden molds, where it supposedly hardened into solid rock. Other researchers, citing an abundance of archaeological evidence, dispute Davidovits's claim that the pyramids are "plastic megaliths," even as newer theories crop up.

Among the latest is that of Thomas J. Crowder, a manpower-planning specialist and amateur Egyptologist, who argues that the pyramids were built with the aid of hydraulic power harnessed from a second Nile River, one that flowed underground. Crowder believes that Egyptian priests stumbled across this hidden

Nile while scouting locations for the pharaoh's underground tomb. After ordering workers to tunnel straight down to the channel and dam it, Crowder contends, the priests were able to divert the river's flow upward right to the construction site.

A kind of retaining wall was then built around the base of the pyramid-to-be to trap the diverted river, and a canal was dug to link it to the nearby Nile. In this way, barges bearing stone blocks could be floated up the canal from the aboveground Nile to the pyramid.

Crowder also maintains that as the pyramid inched skyward, a series of locks was constructed up the structure's angled north wall. By channeling the diverted underground Nile through the pyramid's internal passages and into these locks, engineers were supposedly able to raise a stone-laden barge one lock at a time up the side of the pyramid to the exact level where work was in progress. Once emptied of its cargo, goes the theory, the barge was lowered back down to the moat simply by draining the locks. According to Crowder, these locks remained in place

until the pyramid was complete. They were then dismantled, and the underground Nile was undammed and allowed to return to its former course, unseen and unknown to future generations.

Crowder based his unorthodox theory on a closer reading of the Greek historian Herodotus—specifically on his use of the word *machana* in his account of how the pyramid was built. Traditionally, that Greek word had been translated as "machine," and, as a result, archaeologists have searched for years for some kind of machine the Egyptians might have invented to hoist the stones into place. But machana can also mean "boat," a variance that would not only explain why such a crane has never been found but also buttress Crowder's barge theory.

Most experts discount the second Nile idea. They look to archaeology to find clues to explain the construction of the pyramids. So far, those clues indicate

that the building of the Great Pyramid began when workers cut channels into the bedrock at the site, then filled them with water. Rods were driven into the water-filled channels, and the water line marked on each rod. The rock was then chiseled down to the water line. As primitive as it was, this giant leveling allowed workers to prepare an almost perfectly flat surface to raise a pyramid on.

Similarly simple, and sufficient, were the implements used to quarry the mountain of stone needed for the pharaoh's tomb. Copper saws and chisels, stone mallets, and wooden wedges were among the small handful of tools available to the Egyptian stonemasons who shaped each chunk of quarried rock into a pyramid building block.

Fortunately for the many thousands of laborers on the project, much of the stone that eventually went into building the Great Pyramid was both plentiful and nearby. Unfortunately, in the absence of such labor-saving devices as the wheel, all of that stone still had to be dragged to the site by human sinew, with each block lashed to a wooden sledge that was then ◊

hauled over log rollers using ropes made of plaited reeds. The polished limestone blocks that eventually faced the pyramid had to be floated up the Nile from a quarry ten miles south of Cairo, then dragged the final half-mile from the river to the work site. The granite destined to frame the pharaoh's burial chamber made a similar, albeit longer, journey from its quarry 600 miles upriver at Aswan.

All that dragging did not end at the work site, since each stone still had to be hauled up the side of the pyramid and heaved into final position. The archaeological evidence suggests that one or more ramps were built for this purpose, the ramps eventually reaching to the very top of the pyramid. Once the structure's sandstone cap was in place, the masons worked their way down again, finishing the pyramid in its limestone veneer and dismantling the ramps as they went along.

In all, as many as 150,000 laborers may have poured out their sweat on the Great Pyramid in the name of their god-king, working every year, for as long as thirty years, during the three to four months of late summer when the Nile flooded and they were idled from their jobs in the fields.

Even before those workers had nudged the Great Pyramid's last stone into place, other structures were taking shape on the plateau at Giza. Eventually the Great Pyramid would stand as the centerpiece of a magnificent complex of temples and tombs that would one day rank among the Seven Wonders of the ancient world.

Today, the ruins of that complex are the last of the Seven Wonders that remain, a mecca for tourists and a perennial source of mystery, shrouded as much in myth as they are in the desert haze. □

Egypt's Royal Puzzle

What looks like the work of a master weaver is actually the floor plan of one of ancient Egypt's grandest structures. This complex labyrinth, built in about 2000 BC for the pharaoh Amenemhet III near his pyramid at Fayoum, had two levels, 3,000 rooms, and an enigmatic tangle of dark passages. The historian Herodotus noted that it cost more in money and labor than "all the works and buildings of the Greeks put together."

The maze housed tombs of kings—and of sacred crocodiles—but no one is sure why the sepulchres required such an intricate setting. The labyrinth may have reflected no more than a royal fondness for puzzles. □

Petra: The City of the Dead

Even today, the road to the ruins of Jordan's rose-tinted city of Petra can be traveled only on foot or on horseback along a path that is no more than three feet wide in places. The path winds beneath towering cliffs of pink sandstone that are an impressive prologue for the drama to come: After one last turn, the road becomes a valley whose rocky western wall has been sculpted into a ninety-foot-tall temple, with porticoes, porches, and windows that back onto nothing at all, just like a theater set.

The mysterious temple is called the Pharaoh's Treasury, although no pharaoh ever set foot in it. It was built for some forgotten reason about 2,000 years ago by a nomadic desert people called the Nabataeans. An urn, carved into the rock above the temple and bearing the scars of hundreds of bullets, helps explain the Treasury's name. The urn, says a legend, held a pharaoh's treasure, making the stone vessel a tempting target for passing Bedouins who hoped a lucky shot would pay off in a shower of gold.

Startling as it is, the Pharaoh's Treasury is only one of a number of carved curiosities found near the ruins of Petra. Nearby, for example, stands the palace, and cut into a mountain overlooking the valley looms the Deir, or monastery *(above)*. Like the Pharaoh's Treasury, both are mostly facade, with only a single room behind their elegantly carved pediments, columns, and scrollwork.

In this same eerie complex are

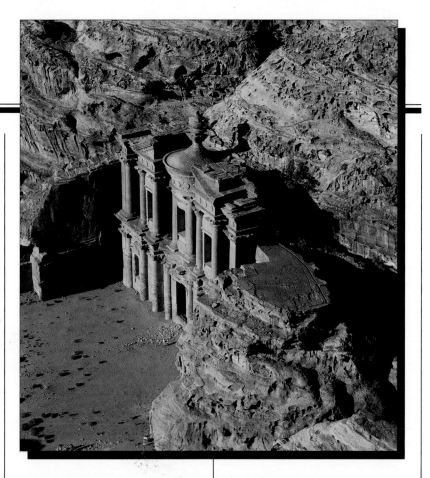

the remains of a Roman theater, its thirty-three tiers of seats hewed from a wall of rock that was already pocked with hundreds of Nabataean tombs when the Romans incorporated Petra into their empire in AD 106. Some of the tombs open onto the theater's uppermost row. From the stage, the scene is one of grim contrast, with rows of seats for 3,000 living spectators and, above and all around them, the resting places of the dead.

More tombs line the road to the city of Petra itself, once the crossroads of the region's great trade routes and home to more than 20,000 people. But a shift in those trade routes sidetracked Petra sometime in the third century, and a devastating earthquake silenced the city forever in AD 350. □

Successive Suez Canals

The present Suez Canal is not the original. Such a waterway was started by the Egyptians around 1800 BC and much later was finished by conquering Romans. The Byzantines neglected it during their period of hegemony in the region, but the Arabs dredged it open again in the seventh century AD. Their labor was wasted, however, since the Ottomans filled it in for military reasons in the year 775. Thereafter, no water route linked the Mediterranean and the Red Sea until the modern canal was completed in 1869. □

Malta's Mysterious Echo Chamber

The word in Greek means "subterranean chamber," but this scarcely describes the marvels of Malta's Hypogeum, a vast complex of more than twenty natural and man-made caverns. Some 4,500 years ago, the Hypogeum was probably a sanctuary—and was certainly a tomb.

In this lightless temple deep underground, worshipers may once have huddled, surrounded perhaps by the bones of their own ancestors, while the voice of an unseen oracle resounded from chamber to chamber. Research has revealed that the Hypogeum is a superb echo chamber that will transmit any deep, low voice from one end of the vault to the other. The speaker has only to sit in a small niche off the so-called Oracle Room and talk, and the words rumble along a ridge cut into the rock below the ceiling and bounce eerily from wall to wall.

That ceiling ridge would seem to denote a prehistoric knowledge of acoustics, and its uncanny sound effects must have been compelling to the prehistoric Maltese who gathered there in order to seek the counsel of the oracle. But the chiseled molding is not the Hypogeum's only archaeological embellishment. Elsewhere within it are decorative spirals painted in red ocher on the ceilings and, in one room, traces of a black-and-white checkerboard pattern on the wall. Many of the rooms feature elaborately carved pillars, doorways, and window niches.

All these carvings—indeed, the entire Hypogeum itself—had to be hewed from solid limestone by workers using only the antler picks and stone mallets of the third millennium BC. The backbreaking task took centuries. Eventually, the Hypogeum encompassed three levels—the lowest thirty feet below the ground—and a disorienting maze of rooms, passages, and stairways. The rooms, some archaeologists believe, constituted a temple devoted to the worship of a goddess. In time, however, the temple apparently became a tomb; it is believed to have held the remains of 6,000 to 7,000 people. Later still, the Hypogeum was inexplicably abandoned. Its dead kept their secret until 1902, when workers cutting cisterns for new houses accidentally broke through the roof of the Hypogeum and flooded its chambers with daylight for the first time in centuries. □

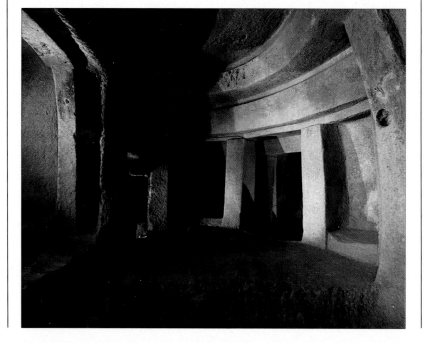

Greeks directed by the engineer Eupalinus built a tunnel more than half a mile long through rock on the island Samos in the sixth century BC. Work started from either side of the mountain, and, although they had only the crudest surveying equipment, the tunnelers managed to meet almost exactly in the middle.

Blueprints in Stone

Scholars have long known that the architects of classical Greece made meticulous plans of the temples and monuments that would become their claims to fame. None of those designs was thought to have survived, however, until 1979, when a set of ancient "blueprints" for the Temple of Apollo at Didyma turned up right under some archaeologists' noses. The plans were etched into the marble walls of the temple itself. Covering hundreds of square yards, they depicted individual parts of the temple in exact 1:1 scale.

Ironically, the plans survived because they were never brought to full fruition. Begun some 2,000 years ago, construction of the temple at Didyma crept along for 600 years, then halted short of completion. Had the temple been finished, final polishing of its marble would have obliterated every trace of the inscribed blueprints. □

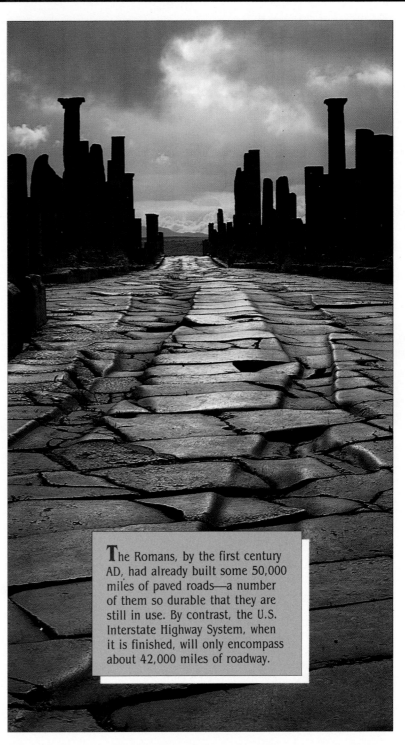

The Romans, by the first century AD, had already built some 50,000 miles of paved roads—a number of them so durable that they are still in use. By contrast, the U.S. Interstate Highway System, when it is finished, will only encompass about 42,000 miles of roadway.

A menacing deity with both human and jaguar features glowers from a 3,500-year-old adobe wall at Huaca de los Reyes in the Andes Mountains of Peru.

A New World Older than Anyone Knew

Historians have long believed that no ancient American society rivaled in achievement or complexity Mesopotamia and Egypt, the great cultural cradles of the Old World. But in the 1980s, archaeologists discovered otherwise.

Working in the fifty or more narrow river valleys that crisscross the Andes along the length of Peru, they found evidence of architecture on a grand scale—towering pyramids and temples, secular buildings, plazas, and private homes—all in planned communities dating back to between 5,000 and 3,500 years ago. This is about the same time that the pyramids were being built in Egypt, and the city-states of Sumer were reaching their peak in Mesopotamia.

"This idea of the Old World being ahead of the New World has to be put on hold," according to Yale archaeologist Richard Burger, one of the antiquarians working on the Andean project. The experts do not contend that the old Peruvian civilization ever matched all the achievements of the ancient Middle East, where writing arose and crucial inventions such as the wheel were created. There is no evidence that the river valley Andean people had a written language or used the wheel—nor did their descendants, including the creative Inca. Even so, the scholars say, the new finds indicate that in the areas of planning, engineering, organization, political sophistication, and creative artistry, the vanished civilization of Peru compared favorably to the Old World cultures.

The Andean finds, adobe structures that have been admirably preserved by the cold, dry mountain climate, include a stepped pyramid more than ten stories tall and an equally lofty U-shaped temple. There were also large secular buildings, storehouses, and plazas—one of them two-thirds of a mile long—flanked by residential areas. Dramatic friezes, their myriad colors still intact, adorn some buildings. The communities apparently lived and lived well on crops grown on nearby irrigated farms.

Many of the ruins, scattered among scores of sites, had only been partially excavated as the 1990s approached, and it seemed likely that the Andean project would yield still more wonders. From what they had already learned, however, archaeologists reasoned that the people who built the Andean towns were politically cohesive and relied on economic cooperation—factors that could explain their ability to mobilize the talent and labor to plan and build on a monumental scale.

Along with casting doubt on the idea of Old World supremacy, the Andean finds have called into question the long-held notion that the Maya, who flourished in Central America, had created the seminal culture of the western hemisphere. The largest of the Andean monuments predate the rise of the Maya by nearly two millennia. □

The Stone Puzzles of the Inca

Although they had neither the wheel nor draft animals and had only the simplest of tools, Incan craftsmen were surpassingly skillful at working with huge blocks of stone. As a result, Incan walls and buildings are masterpieces of construction, with each stone so precisely and painstakingly fitted to adjoining stones that very often even a razor blade cannot be slipped between the joints. Moreover, this remarkably tight fit was achieved without the use of any mortar whatever.

Without mortar, ordinary stonemasons might have relied on gravity, and on the great weight and size of their raw materials, to hold their handiwork together. Incan stonemasons, however, were anything but ordinary. Although they worked with stones weighing as much as 200 tons and standing as tall as twenty-eight feet, they apparently refused to place their trust in even so faithful a force as gravity. Instead, they carved each stone into a multisided block, leaving a slightly convex projection on each face. A corresponding concave depression would then be chiseled out of the adjacent faces of blocks that were already in position in a wall.

It was a lengthy and laborious process of trial and error. Each block had to be repeatedly heaved into place, tested for fit, and then removed—until, finally, it matched up exactly with each of its neighbors. The end result was that each course of stones locked into the ones above and below it with uncanny, jigsaw precision, virtually guaranteeing that the wall or building would be able to stand any test of time.

Many of the Incan structures have survived for more than four centuries in a country where earthquakes quickly turn conventional masonry into rubble. The durability of Incan stonework was put to a severe test in 1950 when an earthquake struck the former Incan capital of Cuzco. Buildings swayed, the ground itself heaved and buckled, and when it was all over, 90 percent of the city's edifices had been damaged or destroyed.

Not one Incan-built wall suffered a single crack. □

The Stones of Tiahuanaco

For many centuries, it was the cultural and ceremonial capital of central South America, a city so admired that local Indians later believed it had been built by the gods or a race of giants. In truth, however, the city of Tiahuanaco, which lies about six miles from Lake Titicaca in present-day Bolivia, was the handiwork of an indigenous Andean people.

The people of Tiahuanaco never had a written language and thus left no written account of themselves. Only Indian legends and the silent stones of the ruined city itself bear witness to a population that may once have numbered 40,000, many of them skilled artisans and knowledgeable farmers. The ruins speak of a brilliant civilization that 2,000 years ago built a city that was a model of urban planning, whose engineers devised a drainage and sewage system that was centuries ahead of its time

and transformed huge blocks of stone into buildings that were at once majestic and mysterious. Among these structures are the Temple of the Sun, whose walls contain many large stones weighing up to 150 tons, and the Gateway of the Sun, which was hewed from a single block of hard andesite.

Yet the people of Tiahuanaco had no harnessed animals and no wheels, not even a roller, and not a single tool made out of anything but stone or bronze. Moreover, there were no quarries or scattered boulders nearby with which to

build such a city. So where did the stones of Tiahuanaco come from, and how did they get here?

A Jesuit priest writing in the days of the Spanish conquest claimed that the stones "were carried through the air to the sound of a trumpet." Actually, they were dragged to their destination and dragged for some distance: ◊

Archaeologists have determined that the quarries that furnished the stones lay anywhere from six to 200 miles away. Some of the stones may have been ferried across Lake Titicaca on totora-reed boats to a port fourteen miles from Tiahuanaco, then hauled overland to the construction site. Once there, the stones were painstakingly chiseled and polished down to an accuracy of one-fiftieth of an inch and fitted together with consummate skill.

That skill is just as apparent at Tiahuanaco's satellite city, Lukurmata, where a temple complex contains stones whose corners are perfectly squared, implying a remarkable knowledge of geometry on the part of some forgotten engineer or stonemason. Some of the stones also have markings on them, perhaps to show workers where and how to place them. If the markings were, in fact, directions, it is possible that the blocks were prefitted and the buildings, in effect, prefabricated.

The temples of Lukurmata and Tiahuanaco, like the cities themselves, feature an ingenious drainage system, one that continues to keep the temple floors dry some 2,000 years after it was installed.

Unfortunately for the people of Tiahuanaco, their empire proved to be shorter-lived than their drainage system. Sometime around AD 1200, the empire slipped into irreversible decline; within fifty years, once-thriving Tiahuanaco was a dead city. To this day, no one can explain its demise. It has since been devastated by earthquakes, pillaged by treasure hunters, and, ironically, used as a quarry, its stone buildings and sculptures scavenged for reuse in building local churches and haciendas. □

Superfarms of the Andes

On the long plain stretching into Peru and Bolivia from 12,000-foot-high Lake Titicaca, the land is mostly pasture now, marked with corrugated strips of alternately high and low ground. Called *waru waru* by the local Indians, these undulating patterns of raised earthen platforms and shallow canals have been all but erased by time and the elements.

Rediscovered in the 1960s, the rippled patches at one time blanketed some 200,000 acres and were believed to be the work of the Inca who farmed there four or five centuries ago. More recent archaeological studies, however, have revealed that the system is in fact an agricultural design, perfected more than 2,500 years ago, that has the ability to outperform modern farming techniques.

At the heart of the system are the earthen platforms *(opposite, above)*, about 3 feet high, 30 to 300 feet long, and 10 to 30 feet wide. These elevated earthworks are separated by canals of similar dimensions and built out of the excavated soil. Over time, the platforms were fertilized periodically with organic silt and nitrogen-rich algae scooped up from the bottom of the canals during the dry season. Even today, more than 500 years after the fields fell idle, the sediment in the old canals is much richer in nutrients than the soil of the surrounding plains.

But the platform-canal system was not merely a way of enriching infertile ground. It also appears to have created a climate that both extended the high-altitude growing season and helped crops survive hard times. During the area's frequent periods of drought, for example, the canals provided vital moisture, while the higher level of the platforms raised plants above the worst effects of the region's frequent floods. Moreover, the canal water may have acted as a kind of thermal storage battery, absorbing the sun's heat during the day and radiating it back into the freezing night, to create a blanket of relatively warm air over the growing plants.

In 1981, archaeologists began to reconstruct some of the ancient raised fields, using tools, techniques, and crops similar to those used by the original farmers. Over the first five years of the experiment, the raised fields consistently yielded three times more potatoes—a time-honored Andean staple—than did conventional plots.

The resurrected technology also performed well in the harsh climate of the high Andes. A severe frost that devastated nearby farms in 1982 did little damage to the experimental fields. The following year the crops on the elevated platforms survived an equally ruinous drought, then rode high and dry through a 1986 flood that swamped surrounding farmlands.

Impressed by these results, the government of Peru and international development agencies are paying farmers to repair the waru waru and to put them back into production. Farmers elsewhere in Latin America are also experimenting with the old technique of raised-platform farming. ☐

Sanctuaries in the Clouds

High in the Andes, a mile or more above the elevations of permanent settlements, archaeologists have discovered scores of ruined structures that present-day South American Indians call *huacas,* or holy places. Scattered along the spine of the Andes from Peru to Chile, the ruins are mostly rows of stones or low walls, although some are more elaborately equipped with altarlike platforms and outdoor shelters. One has been found at an elevation of 22,000 feet, nearly two miles above the level where airplane pilots must don oxygen masks. It is believed to be the world's highest structure.

No one knows who built the sanctuaries or precisely how they were used. Ritual offerings of dolls, statues, coca leaves, and food—and even evidence of human sacrifice—have been found at some sites, seeming to confirm the religious significance of the shrines. Some researchers see a link with Incan sun worship in the orientation of the structures; they also detect the skilled hand of Incan engineers in the high-altitude constructions.

But others associate the shattered huacas with rituals that predate the Inca. In this view, the difficult climb to such heights, the exhausting labor, and the vanished ceremonies that were once performed there were efforts to gain favor with meteorological gods—of a so-called water cult that persists even today among the people of the high, dry Andes. ☐

The mummified remains of this Incan child, sacrificed to the sun 500 years ago, were discovered in 1954 at a shrine on the peak of 17,712-foot El Plomo Mountain (*background*).

Chimor's Quest for Water

The Chimu of pre-Columbian Peru were scientifically unsophisticated by many measures, but their struggle to survive in one of the world's driest coastal deserts spurred them on to prodigious feats of hydraulic engineering.

Some of their knowledge of water management was inherited from their predecessors, the Mochica people, who inhabited Peru's Moche Valley during the first millennium AD and built a network of so-called great trenches to irrigate their fields. By the time the Chimu came on the scene around AD 1100, however, shifts in the earth's crust had permanently separated many of those early canals from the rivers that fed them.

In an effort to thwart the effects of terrestrial buckling, Chimu engineers devised sophisticated gravity-fed canals that hugged the contours of the land and provided just enough slope to maintain a con-

stant flow of water. Movable sluice gates were installed in order to further control the flow of water from the main canals to the distribution lines.

Eventually, the Chimu canal system would comprise hundreds of miles of waterways. Earthen aqueducts, some of them almost 30 feet high and close to 2,000 feet long, were constructed to carry water across canyons. Elaborate terraces were built up along mountainsides to bring the canals across the Andean foothills.

The construction and maintenance of this network was funded by a labor tax levied on the people of Chimor, while the manpower was recruited from the kingdom's large lower class. Work gangs used stone and bronze tools to build the canals, chiseling through solid rock in some places. An ingenious ceramic surveying device *(below)*, remarkably similar to today's the-

odolite, allowed the system's architects to plot the best routes through terrain that would challenge modern engineers equipped with the latest technology.

As it turned out, however, even the contour canals were no match for tectonic uplift, the inexorable rising of the earth's crust. Like the great trenches before them, the canals were in constant need of repair. In addition, unusually heavy rainfalls—the result of cyclical El Niño climate disturbances that as recently as 1982 dumped ninety inches of rain on the area in a single week—destroyed large sections of the canals, necessitating massive reconstruction.

But rebuilding the canals also gave the system's engineers the opportunity to redesign them. As a result, many were straightened and lined with stones to improve their hydraulic efficiency and reduce the effects of erosion. Some were also rebuilt with trapezoid channels—a design that minimized the friction of the flowing water.

Despite these innovations, tectonic uplift continued to strand some of the canals, eventually forcing their abandonment. In a desperate effort to replenish the system's water supply, the Chimu decided to tap the Chicama River, located some fifty miles north of their capital city of Chan Chan. They built a new waterway, now called the Intervalley Canal, to funnel the river's water into the existing canal system.

Over the next century, as many as 5,000 people may have toiled away whole lifetimes on the project, even rebuilding some sections of the unfinished canal four times in order to correct for tectonic uplift. But the rising of the terrain outpaced these efforts, and the builders finally called off the construction of the Intervalley Canal sometime around the year 1300. Work never resumed. Even though the canal had almost been completed, not one drop of water ever trickled through its stone-lined channel. □

Europe's Glass Fortresses

No one knows for certain how it happened, but dozens of ancient forts in Europe were at some point subjected to such intense heat that their stone walls melted and fused into a solid, glassy mass.

Most of these so-called vitrified forts are located in Scotland, although a few have been found in England, France, and Germany. Some, such as Scotland's Tap O' North, are huge, with walls twenty feet thick enclosing thousands of square yards, and are placed strategically on hilltops. Others, including the ring forts of Rahoy and Langwell, are tiny enclosures encompassing fewer than two hundred square yards. Many of these fortresses date from as early as the seventh century BC, although others were built centuries later.

Regardless of location, size, or age, all these forts have one thing in common: They were once engulfed by flames that reached blast-furnace temperatures of at least 2,000 degrees Fahrenheit and virtually melted the rock.

Some archaeologists have speculated that the glass forts were produced by mischance. According to this theory, the forts' walls may have been framed with timbers that were accidentally ignited by sparks from domestic fires. But given the large number of vitrified forts, it is difficult to believe that the prehistoric people who built them could have been so habitually careless with fire.

A more likely scenario is that the walls were built around a core of timbers and then intentionally torched, perhaps by invaders who piled brush and trees against the ramparts and set them on fire. However, as experiments have shown, such fires would have had to rage for many hours, if not days, to generate the hellish heat needed to vitrify stone—time ◊

This reconstruction of a Chimu surveying instrument shows how canal-building Peruvians may have calculated the slope of the land to achieve the most efficient water flow. The device consisted of a ceramic bowl pierced by a hollow sighting tube passing through a calibrated, cross-shaped opening (inset). An artificial horizon was established by aligning water with the three dots in the bowl, which was leveled in a larger, sand-filled vessel atop a tripod (far left); when the sighting tube was in the center of the cross-shaped opening it was parallel to the artificial horizon. Chimu surveyors marked a rod at the height of the level sighting tube, then moved the rod a known distance along uneven ground and sighted the mark. The ground slope corresponded to the tube angle indicated by the calibrations inside the bowl.

enough, say detractors of this theory, for all but the dullest-witted defenders to douse the flames, and time enough for survivors of such a battle to redesign their forts to make them less vulnerable to fire.

On the other hand, the fires may have been set by the builders of the forts themselves, perhaps to strengthen their defenses by fusing piled stone into a solid, glassy shield. This would explain why some forts appear to have been designed with vitrification in mind and why that design persisted for a thousand years or more. But it still leaves open the question of how the forts were vitrified, a riddle even modern scientists have so far been unable to solve. □

The Megalithic Mysteries

Europe in general, and Britain and France in particular, are dotted with prehistoric megalithic monuments—hulking slabs of stone, rising solitary in the landscape in many cases, but sometimes arranged in circles, lines, or clusters. Among the most mysterious and surely the most widely known of the megalithic sites is Stonehenge, the haunting ring of stone that has dominated England's Salisbury Plain for almost five millennia.

According to a number of legends, magic played a role in Stonehenge's creation: The wizard Merlin raised the stones through sorcery, one fanciful story goes. But the truth, archaeologists now surmise, is actually more remarkable than any of the numerous fictions. Stonehenge, they assert, represents the sweat of generations of ancient Britons, with the work spread over some 1,200 years and across the backs of hundreds of laborers at any one time.

Studies have revealed that the monument was built in three stages, the first beginning around 3000 BC, when surveyors pegged one end of a 160-foot rope to the ground and tied a pointed stake to the other end to make an enormous compass. By stretching the rope taut and dragging the stake over the turf as they walked along, the surveyors were able to draw what is today Stonehenge's great outer circle. In their wake came teams of laborers who used deer-antler picks and ox-bone shovels to turn the scribed line into a ditch rimmed on either side by banks of excavated earth and chalk.

Inside the innermost bank, the workers dug a second circle consisting of fifty-six pits, each two to six feet across and some two to four feet deep. These so-called Aubrey Holes, named for their seventeenth-century discoverer, were later found to contain cremated human remains, leading some researchers to the obvious conclusion that the holes had been burial pits. Other people claim, however, that stone or wooden markers inserted in the holes could be used to calculate eclipses of the sun and the moon. The Heel Stone, a thirty-five-ton hunk of sarsen, was also heaved into place at this time, one hundred feet outside Stonehenge's entranceway, where it stands to this day as a lone sentinel.

The second phase of construction got under way around 2000 BC, when about eighty more standing stones were erected in two rows to form a half circle within the perimeter of Stonehenge's outer circle. What distinguishes these stones, however, is not their size—they weigh a paltry four tons compared to the thirty-five-ton Heel Stone—but their composition. They are made of volcanic bluestone, a type of rock found only in Wales, more than 130 miles away, and only in a one-square-mile area of the Prescelly Mountains.

According to archaeologists, after the stones were cut free from their Welsh quarry, they were tied to wooden sledges and hauled about fifteen miles to the sea over a path of log rollers. The stones were then transferred to rafts and ferried along the Welsh coast and up a series of rivers, eventually reaching the river Avon and the edge of the Salisbury Plain. There they were unloaded and dragged the final ten miles or so to the construction site.

But even that culturally jarring feat pales in comparison to the amount of energy that was expended in the third phase of construction, which began with the removal of the bluestone pillars around 1500 BC. Afterward, more than eighty huge sarsen stones, some weighing fifty tons, were hauled about twenty miles from the quarry site at Avebury to Stonehenge, a task that is estimated to have taken 1,000 people seven full years to accomplish.

Many, if not all, of those stones had already been roughly shaped before the journey to Stonehenge.

The shaping process probably involved setting fire to a line of fat-soaked twigs laid atop a stone, then splashing the hot strip of rock with cold water. This, together with synchronized bashing with stone mauls, was often enough to cause the stone to split apart. Final shaping and polishing took place at the construction site, where stonemasons used sarsen mauls to pound away any imperfections and shape the mortises and tenons that would join the horizontal lintels to their corresponding uprights. At the estimated rate of six cubic inches per hour, this job alone would have consumed half a million man-hours of labor. Even so, the stones still had to be sanded smooth —by using other sarsens as gigantic files—and even then the work was far from over. For each up-right, a deep hole had to be dug with three straight sides and the fourth side sloped to form a ramp. As many as 200 people then tilted each stone into its hole, easing it down the ramp and using log levers to pry it upright.

The process of capping each set of uprights with a lintel was no less exacting. Each seven-ton lintel was laid on the ground alongside the uprights, then levered upward inches at a time at each end while workers shoved logs underneath. Once the tower of logs had risen to the thirteen-foot level of the uprights, the lintel was shifted sideways so that its mortises slipped over the projecting tenons of the uprights.

When it was finally completed, sometime after 1600 BC, Stonehenge boasted five trilithons, or three-stone groupings, each consisting of two uprights crowned with a single lintel, surrounded by an unbroken ring of uprights and lintels. The bluestones that had been removed earlier were also replaced, with some of them forming a horseshoe inside the trilithons and others composing a circle between the trilithons and the outer ring of stones.

Nearly 1.5 million man-hours of labor had gone into building Stonehenge, and whole generations of early Britons had lived, labored, and died within its lengthening shadow. Today, almost 5,000 years later, the end result of all that labor still stands, still commanding admiration and awe. □

Shaping the Earth

Just seventeen miles from Stonehenge stands a mystery to rival those riddles in stone: a man-made mountain, 130 feet high and 4,500 years old, known for centuries as Silbury Hill.

Old stories say that the mountain owes its name to a certain King Sil, who, after his death, was propped up on a horse made of gold and then entombed in an estimated 36,000,000 basketfuls of earth—a task that may have kept some 500 people busy for fifteen years or more.

The project was not only gargantuan, it was also fairly precise. From a base covering five acres, workers skillfully constructed the mound in stairstep fashion, like a wedding cake, then smoothed it over with still more dirt.

Despite tales of the gold horse that lay within, the hill was left untouched until the modern era; plunderers were no doubt discouraged by the need to bore through so much earth. Not until 1776 was a shaft sunk into Silbury Hill. But neither King Sil nor his golden steed was found on that occasion. A second tunnel in 1849 fared no

better, nor did an even more ambitious effort in 1968. In fact, all of the digging has yet to produce a single convincing clue to explain why so many people might have worked so hard for so long to create a mound that had no defensive use nor, apparently, any other utilitarian purpose.

There are many theories about what the mound's builders might have intended—a giant sundial, perhaps, or a huge symbol of an eye or a monument to some long-forgotten deity. For now, however, Silbury Hill, the tallest prehistoric structure in Europe, reveals no more about its makers than their capacity for epic feats of labor. □

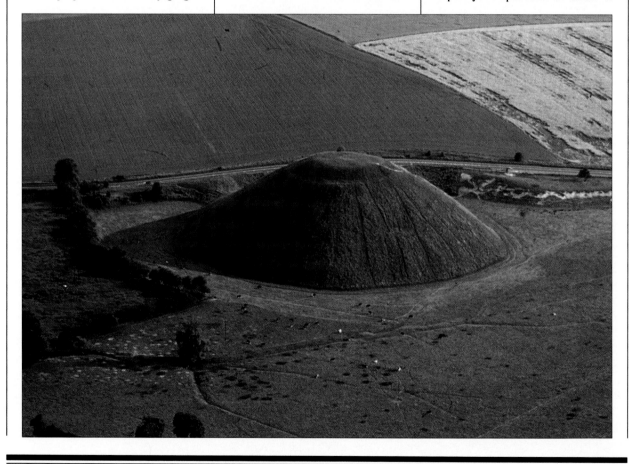

Sri Lanka's Life-Sustaining Wewas

The problem facing the people of ancient Sri Lanka was one of too much too soon: too much rain in too short a time. During the two yearly monsoon seasons that lasted a total of seven months, most of the island virtually drowned in rain. The remainder of the year, drought threatened to destroy the vital rice crop.

The solution was an ambitious system of dams, canals, and storage tanks—called *wewas*—designed to trap the monsoon rains for timed release during the dry season. This approach was not easily achieved, since Sri Lankans of the first century AD had only the simplest of tools.

Nevertheless, the system was built—and rebuilt and enlarged and repaired over many generations. By the time the twelfth-century king Parakramabahu I *(right)* officially decreed that not one drop of water should reach the sea without first serving humanity, his tiny kingdom was already studded with thousands of wewas.

The tanks were fed by tapping and trapping almost every natural source of water available, often by means of massive earthen dams. In turn, the wewas supplied the rice fields of practically every village through a vast network of canals and underground channels.

One tank, the Padawiya, built during the fifth century, was capable of holding fifteen miles of water. Another, at the Madura River, fed millions of tons of water through six-mile-long sluices into a series of smaller reservoirs. Some of the stone blocks used in its construction were thirty-three feet long and weighed fifteen tons.

Time, wars, and the encroaching jungle were later to claim many of the tanks. But some are still used today; others are being restored. Perhaps not surprisingly, the spots picked by modern engineers as optimum for water control are almost invariably the same sites where the ancients built. □

The Bronze Age Manhattan

It should never have been there, reasoned archaeologists, sure that no full-fledged civilization could have existed in Pakistan's Indus River valley 4,500 years ago. But there Mohenjo-Daro was, an entire city, centuries ahead of its time and remarkably preserved beneath the very layer of silt that may have contributed to its downfall.

The city was discovered by accident in 1922, when an Indian archaeologist, intent on probing the remains of a Buddhist temple, dug deep and found, in addition to the temple, the relics of a prehistoric civilization. Teams of archaeologists descended on the area and gradually unearthed the outlines of a carefully planned metropolis *(above),* complete with paved streets, stately brick civic centers, and rows of brick townhouses served by indoor plumbing and an extensive sewage system.

The antiquarians could thank Mohenjo-Daro's location for the city's superb state of preservation; it had been built on the mound that inspired its name—which in the local Sindhi dialect means "Hill of the Dead." The hill was thought to be bewitched, causing anyone who dared climb it to turn a bright blue, and fear of this fate had been enough to keep away the curious for centuries.

In its heyday around 2000 BC, Mohenjo-Daro was home to some 40,000 people, and together with its sister-city, Harappa, located 350 miles away, embodied the strength of an empire that flourished for five centuries.

The heart of Mohenjo-Daro was its citadel, a walled complex of assembly halls and administrative offices. Nearby stood a huge communal bath, along with a civic granary that featured an ingenious air-circulation system that was apparently designed to keep stored grain from spoiling.

Below the citadel a dozen arrow-straight streets carved the city into a north-south grid that was then sliced into blocks by somewhat narrower east-west streets. It was this layout that prompted archaeologists to dub the city the "Bronze Age Manhattan," so closely did the grid resemble the straightforward arrangement of the New York City borough.

Shops, food stands, and look-alike, two-story houses—all built of brick, like almost everything else in Mohenjo-Daro—crowded the streets. Inside the houses, bedrooms, passageways, and guest rooms clustered around central courtyards. Many of the houses also had indoor brick-lined wells, and almost every house had its own bathroom, which included a brick-paved shower stall and a brick, sit-down toilet.

Water for these facilities was hand-carried, of course, in the absence of any system for piping it into the houses. However, there was a system of chutes and clay pipes to carry the runoff from the bathrooms into brick-lined sewage drains that ran alongside each main street. Manholes with removable stone covers were located at each intersection to make it easier for sanitation workers to clean and maintain the entire system.

Given the city's seeming passion for cleanliness and order, it is ironic that water may have played a part in Mohenjo-Daro's decline.

Archaeological evidence suggests that the residents fought a protracted battle against floods. Indeed, parts of Mohenjo-Daro may have been rebuilt as many as eight times, and its citizens were apparently as exacting as they were tenacious. With each rebuilding, the city appears to have been reconstructed in brick-for-brick detail.

But its citizens' determination proved unavailing in the end.

Sometime in the eighteenth century BC, Mohenjo-Daro faded from history—perhaps, ultimately, at the point of an invader's sword. Archaeologists have uncovered in the city's ruins a number of skeletons whose skulls bear the telltale scars of sword cuts.

Time and nature did the rest, silting over the city and burying it beneath the rubble of its own extraordinary brickwork. □

The Monster Stones of Baalbek

Near the modern Lebanese city of Baalbek—a place the Greeks and Romans called Heliopolis, or City of the Sun—there once ran an ancient trade route linking Damascus and Tyre. At this site, Roman engineers in the first century AD raised a spectacular temple complex that seemed designed to dazzle passing caravans with the empire's power and splendor. The complex was dominated by the magnificent Temple of Jupiter, a stone colossus surrounded by a forest of fifty-four columns of immense size and height. Beneath the temple lay an even greater wonder: a huge foundation called the Grand Terrace, comprising an area of more than five million square feet and containing more stone—all precisely cut and fitted—than the Great Pyramid of Khufu. Not one ounce of mortar was used in its construction; yet, in twenty centuries, the Grand Terrace has not settled a single millimeter.

The secret of the Grand Terrace's remarkable stability may lie in one of its retaining walls, which contains three of the world's biggest blocks of cut stone. Stood upright, each would be as tall as a five-story building, and each weighs more than 600 tons.

Together, these three stones compose the Trilithon—and one of the world's oldest mysteries: To this day, no one can convincingly explain how the builders of Baalbek managed to move these monstrous slabs of rock from their quarry almost a mile away, let alone how these dauntless workers might have lifted the stones twenty feet above the ground in order to nudge them into position. It was a job that even today would tax the most sophisticated equipment.

The mystery is only deepened by the presence of a fourth, even larger, stone, cut but then abandoned in the quarry *(left).* At almost 1,100 tons and seventy-two feet long, the so-called Monolith is the largest piece of hewn rock on the face of the earth. To budge it an inch would have required an army of more than 16,000 workers, all pulling in unison. Moreover, as far as anyone today knows, no machine of its time could have lifted the Monolith. Indeed, the technology to move so massive an object would not appear for another 2,000 years, with the development of an enormous tracked crawler of the sort NASA used to transport the Saturn V rocket from its assembly building to its launching pad at Cape Canaveral. □

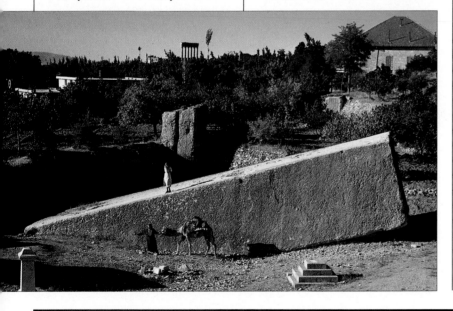

The Venice of the South Pacific

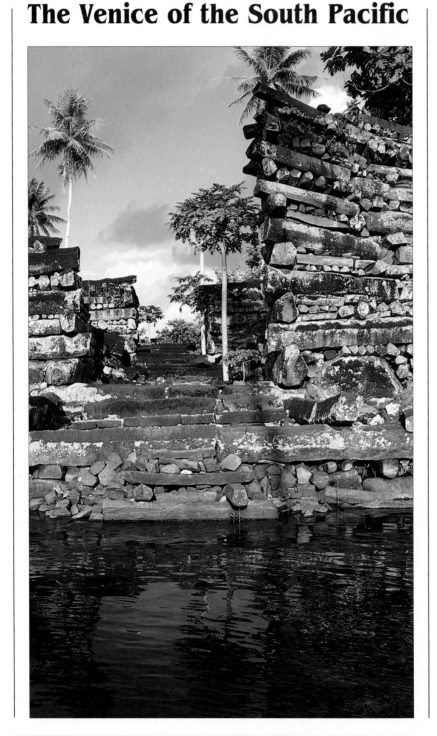

Dangling off the eastern coast of the mountainous volcanic island of Pohnpei in the South Pacific is a necklace of ninety-two artificial islets. They rest in a shallow lagoon, interlaced with waterways and separated from the ocean surf by a pair of giant sea walls. The islets make up a Venicelike city called Nan Madol, which various legends have said was built by Spanish pirates or was once the capital of a vast oceanic empire or is all that remains of the mythical lost continent of Mu.

In fact, Nan Madol was built some 800 years ago, not by pirates or by advanced beings now extinct, but by native Pohnpeians. It was, moreover, both a center of ritual and a royal enclave, seat of a dynasty of powerful island monarchs called *saudeleurs*—one of whom is remembered chiefly for his fondness for dining on head lice and for his insistence that those subjects who refused to share their cargo of vermin with their king should be put to death.

However barbaric the ruler's dining habits might seem, his engineers were quite sophisticated. At its peak in the sixteenth century, Nan Madol was home to as many as a thousand people, who lived in a style altogether different from that of the island's modern inhabitants. Chief among those early citizens, of course, was the saudeleur himself. He made his home on Pahnkadira Islet, a residential compound the size of three football fields, complete with servants' quarters, bathing pools, and the temple of Nan Zapue, the thunder god.

Like all of Nan Madol's islets, Pahnkadira rests on a stretch of coral reef that was walled in with basalt columns quarried on Pohnpei. Once the walls were in place, the resulting enclosed pool was filled with coral gravel to form a dry platform above sea level. The platform, in turn, was paved over with stones. Some of the Nan Madol islets built in this way rise as high as twenty feet above the surrounding waters, and the walls that enclose them tower as high as thirty feet.

To build the walls that made the islets possible, basalt blocks weighing from five to ten tons each were fractured loose from Pohnpei quarries in a process that involved heating the rock at its base with huge fires, then cooling it rapidly with seawater. Giant slabs were then hauled and floated into place offshore, where they were stacked like logs to form the islets' retaining walls (opposite).

In the residential section of Nan Madol, islanders lived in pole-and-thatch dwellings whose size was determined by the status of the owners. The saudeleur, for example, lived in a house that measured almost 1,500 square feet. Other nobles made do with half as much space, while servants squeezed into tiny huts measuring a mere 60 square feet.

The saudeleur was equally exalted in death. Many of the rulers were buried in the royal mortuary on Nandauwas Islet behind elegantly upswept walls that rose as high as twenty-five feet around a maze of courtyards and crypts.

Nan Madol's glory ended sometime in the 1600s, when, according to tradition, the reigning saudeleur was defeated by an invader from a neighboring island—no less an invader, in fact, than the alleged son of the thunder god. A century or so later, Nan Madol was deserted, and by the time the first Europeans stepped ashore in the 1820s, it was little more than a ghost town, with only its dead to keep watch amid the eerie ruins of its basalt majesty. □

The Great Zimbabwe

Geologist Karl Mauch could hardly believe his eyes as he and his party, exploring in what would later become the British colony of Rhodesia, stepped from the bush one day in 1871. Scattered across the hill and valley in front of him was a network of ruins—edifices expertly worked in stone in a land where primitive mud huts were the norm. The mystery of the place was almost palpable. "Profound silence brooded over the scene," Mauch would later recall of the slumbering enigma called Great Zimbabwe.

Beneath that pall of silence and at the heart of the ruins, Mauch found a huge enclosure with granite walls thirty feet high and twenty feet thick in places (below). This stone enclosure was known to the natives as Mumbahuru, or "the House of the Great Woman," and it did not take Mauch long to succumb to his own wishful thinking and leap to the conclusion that the great woman must be the legendary queen of Sheba. Great Zimbabwe, by the same stretch of the imagination, must have been the capital of her kingdom of Ophir and the site of the fabled mines of the queen's consort, Israel's King Solomon.

But Mauch was wrong, as were the legions of later explorers and historians who concocted other myths of a lost white civilization in the heart of black Africa. The truth, as archaeolo- ◊

gists learned by 1906, was that Great Zimbabwe had once been the trading and religious capital of a black African empire, and parts of it were built as early as the second or third century AD by the ancestors of the very natives who first led Karl Mauch to the site.

Over a period of more than a thousand years, Great Zimbabwe grew from a typical Iron Age settlement of poled huts into a simple walled enclave and finally into a bewildering sixty-acre sprawl of huts, ceremonial shrines, passageways, and granaries. Nowhere in this complex was there a straight wall or a right angle, and nowhere

was any mortar used to bind granite block to granite block *(below)*. Moreover, all of the blocks, including the 15,000 tons of granite used in the so-called Great Enclosure, were laid in bricklike courses, fitted together with precision, and sometimes capped with decorative, chevron-shaped border treatments.

The ruins of the complex are clustered in two main groups, with a smattering of smaller sites in between. The first group is a jumble of natural rock and man-made structures inaccurately dubbed the Hill Fortress. (It was built not for defense but only to impress.) Also called the Acropolis, the complex

stands atop a boulder-strewn, 300-foot-high hill. It is reached by climbing a narrow, twisting stairway that squeezes between outcrops of rock and often allows only one person at a time to pass. Stone walls, punctuated by stone towers, creep from rock to rock and climb uphill and down, creating a labyrinth of enclosures.

Nearby, at the edge of a cliff overlooking the valley, is a cave that acts as a giant amplifier, augmenting the voice of anyone speaking inside and projecting it to the valley below. The cave lends some credence to an ancient tribal legend that tells of an African god-king who ruled from a rocky hilltop. No mere mortal dared look this king in the eye, since the penalty for such effrontery was instant death. The king's cowering subjects were only allowed to hear their master's voice, a voice that was said to echo and reecho, striking terror into all who heard it.

If that king did reign at Great Zimbabwe, he may have made his home across the valley from the Hilltop Fortress in the Great Enclosure itself, a massive, oval-shaped structure that dates to the fourteenth century and was apparently the palace of a great chief. Dominating the Great Enclosure, and built of the same mortarless granite, is a strange conical tower thirty feet high and fifty feet wide at its base. Although it may have had some forgotten religious significance, its function is unknown today. Moreover, that mystery is likely to endure, since the tower is literally rock solid, with no windows or doors to provide access and no distinguishing features of any kind to provide even the slightest clue to its use. □

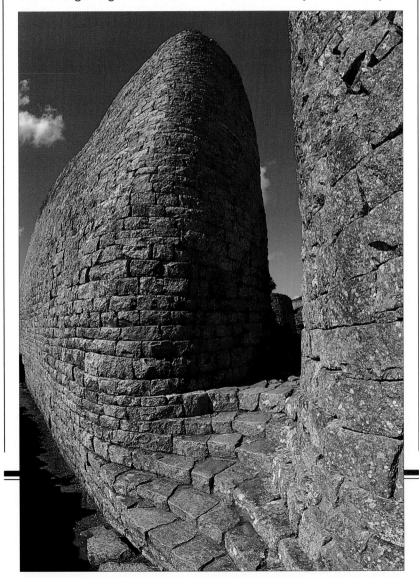

Marked by a flashlight transformed by time exposure into a glowing trail, a road built a thousand years ago by the Anasazi Indians of New Mexico stretches toward the dawn.

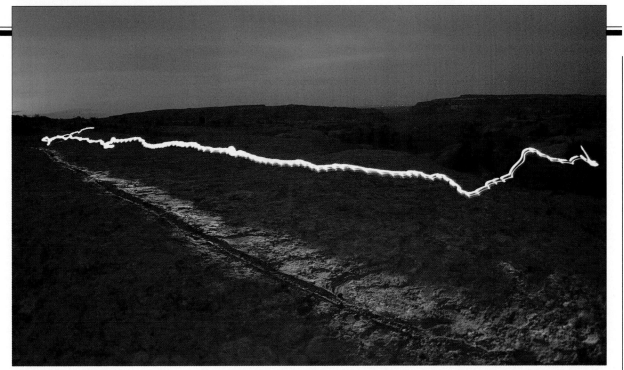

Roads to Nowhere

They were built a thousand years ago by people who knew nothing of the wheel and had never seen a horse. Yet the Anasazi Indian roads of New Mexico were not simple footpaths but a 500-mile network of carefully planned and superbly engineered causeways.

Now worn faint by wind and time, some of the roads were thirty feet wide. Others had stone curbs. And most of them ran arrow straight through mile after dusty mile of barren desert, regardless of the surrounding terrain. Even where a short detour might have offered the road builders a flat surface for their labors, the Anasazi cut steps and ramps into cliffs if necessary to keep their avenues relentlessly linear.

The likeliest-seeming purpose of the highway system would be to link the main Anasazi settlement at Chaco Canyon to its thirty or so satellite communities. But although all the roads do radiate from Chaco Canyon, and some of them do connect with outlying villages, a few lead only to isolated lakes, springs, and mountain peaks. Even more mysterious, in certain places there are two parallel sets of roads.

Most enigmatic of all is the Great North Road, which climbs out of Chaco Canyon and makes a fifty-mile beeline due north across rolling sagebrush country, only to come to a dead end at the edge of another, even more isolated, canyon. With one possible exception, there were no villages along the road's route. Its only apparent purpose was to strike north, and its only apparent destination was a particular mound on the rim of a

particular canyon. But why that mound? And why due north? And why, moreover, should this road to nowhere be littered in places with broken pottery?

The answers may lie in the many Anasazi legends that tell of ritual journeys to sacred mountains and canyons. Similar tales speak of straight roads that lead to *sipapu*, small holes that the Anasazi believed were channels to the spirit world. Clues may also rest with Anasazi rituals in which pottery was ceremoniously shattered to honor the dead.

Some researchers have concluded that a number of the Anasazi roads—the Great North Road in particular—were never meant to go anywhere, at least in the temporal world. Instead, the roads may have been bridges designed to link the real world of Chaco Canyon to an unseen landscape of the spirit. □

The Cuzco Cat

In the fifteenth century AD, Pachacuti, the first Incan conqueror and
ninth of a dynasty of kings, decided to rebuild the 400-year-old capital at Cuzco, located high in the
Peruvian Andes. Monumental buildings were raised around broad plazas, and the banks of the Huatanay
and Tullumayo rivers were paved
with flagstones.

On a crag known as Sacsahuaman, which overlooked the city,
the builders and their legions of
workers fashioned a granite fortress from carefully tailored inter-
locking stones, assembled without
mortar. The three zigzag walls were
made of precisely fitted blocks
weighing as much as 300 tons,
among the largest ever used in
human construction.

But Pachacuti's engineers were
engaged in more than precocious
stonework. To achieve their sover-
eign's grand design for Cuzco, they
used the terrain as a giant canvas
on which to depict a sacred animal; the new city took form within
the stylized body of the beast. The
two rivers flowing through Cuzco
defined a feline body; their junc-
tion south of the city, a tail. Cuzco's broad central plaza was the
creature's heart. The granite fortress on Sacsahuaman became a
ferocious head, its angled walls the
zigzag teeth of a growling jaguar,
drawn in stone. □

ARTISTS

The urge to create works of art has been a driving force in human development since the dawn of time. Archaeologists the world over have uncovered artifacts showing that so-called primitive peoples everywhere felt a deep need to express themselves in some tangible way. What so often surprises us today about their output is its scale and the excellence of its execution, despite the fact that the earliest artists were severely restricted in the tools they had at their disposal.

For the Cro-Magnon, the first modern humans in Europe, the walls of caves became canvases on which they painted panoplies of animals, some of which they depended on for food and clothing. For other prehistoric peoples it was the earth itself that was shaped and manipulated, and in the process of rearranging nature, they produced some of the largest renditions of human and animal forms ever.

Art was magic and power. Anyone who could draw an animal to near perfection must have been seen as a special person, a conjurer. Indeed, the first artists are thought to have been shamans or priests—individuals who could evoke through their work the very spirits of the beasts that they rendered.

Soon, art became a regular part of ceremony and ritual, a way of engendering mystery and supporting belief, and the artists' output in the centuries ahead steadily increased as demand for it grew. And then, with a further blossoming of skills and improvements in technology, art took on another major function. It became the means by which important individuals could impress their gods and fellow mortals in hope of ensuring that their memory would live on through the ages, as with the terra-cotta army of Qin Shi Huangdi *(above)*. Although the names of the patrons have in most instances been lost to time, their monuments survive, now tributes less to any individual's greatness than to human ingenuity and creativity.

Art Ahead of Its Time

"We have invented nothing!" Pablo Picasso reportedly exclaimed as he emerged from France's famed Lascaux Cave. Inside, he had examined some of the most remarkable art in the world. What remains humbling to this day is that it was produced 17,000 years ago.

When the first of the caves containing such prehistoric art came to light in 1868 in Altamira, Spain, incredulous viewers dismissed the paintings as being no more than twenty years old, "the expression of a mediocre student of the modern school." But later discoveries of other painted caves in Spain and France forced a radical reversal of opinion; critics were soon marveling over the artists'

incredible achievements. Only one of these caves would outrival Altamira for pure brilliance, however, and that was Lascaux, accidentally stumbled upon in 1940 by a boy searching for his lost dog.

Here, approximately 600 paintings, almost 1,500 engravings on stone, and many inscrutable dots and geometric forms bedazzle the eye. Across the ceilings and walls flows a cavalcade of animals—aurochs (ancestors of today's oxen), bison, reindeer, horses *(below),*

and other creatures, depicted running, galloping, charging.

Working in semidarkness, with only the light of guttering torches and fat-burning lamps to see by, sitting or standing on rickety scaffolding or out-of-the-way perches, and using the most primitive of tools (often a fingertip for a brush), the geniuses of Lascaux carefully outlined and then colored

in their menagerie. Even after the lapse of millennia, the paintings preserve much of their original brilliance. The reason for this goes beyond the fact that they were sealed away in darkness for so long. Modern analysis of the paints shows that the artists had a deep knowledge of how to prepare pigments for maximum clarity and stability. They ground such naturally occurring substances as iron and manganese oxide with primitive mortars to produce reds, blacks, and yellows, then mixed the powders with water before applying the colors to the walls. But they were not above experimentation, and they tried a variety of other binding agents as well, everything from blood, urine, and fish glue to fat, egg white, and vegetable juices. To bring out just the right tones, they at times subjected the pigments to high heat. The entire process, in some ways, presaged modern chemistry.

More amazingly, the artists grappled with the problem of three dimensionality. They cleverly used natural irregularities in the rock surface to help give the paintings depth; thus a bulge in the wall might become the haunch of an aurochs or the swollen belly of a pregnant bison. By overlapping animals of different sizes, they created a further illusion of depth. And they took pains to provide just the right amount of distance between the front or hind legs of some of their beasts to make it appear as though there were real space between them. In all this, the cave artists were well ahead of their times—so much so, in fact, that many of their techniques would not be duplicated for millennia to come. □

A Show of Hands

The hands of a vanished people seem to wave from the walls of more than twenty caves in northern Spain, Italy, and southwestern France. Stenciled by Cro-Magnon some 25,000 years ago, they are ghostly impressions left by some of the first modern humans. But why the hands are there and what they mean is a puzzle.

Of the caves, the one called Gargas in the French Pyrénées has the most handprints—more than 150 of them—and these range in size from infant to adult. Remarkably, the majority represent left hands. But the truly astonishing aspect of the hands is that almost all of them—including those of small children—seem to be missing parts of their fingers.

Made during the late Ice Age, most of the outlines were sprayed on with earth pigments: ocher for red, manganese dioxide for black. The coloring, either in powdered or liquid form, was probably blown through a tube—possibly a hollow reed or stem—onto the hand as the palm was pressed to the moist wall. This method, experts say, may account for the prevalence of left hands, since the right hand—typically, the more dexterous one—would have held the tube.

What is not clear at all is why so many of the hands appear to be mutilated. Usually missing are the top two joints of at least two fingers. Close study suggests that the joints were actually gone, not merely bent under.

One theory held that because the Cro-Magnon lived during the Ice Age, frostbite, which can lead to gangrene, may have caused the digits to drop off. Even leprosy was considered as a possibility. But a study of strange holes poked in the mud walls and ceiling of a circular chamber in the Gargas Cave indicated otherwise. When the investigator examining the holes made casts of them, he found they had been created by fingers—but instead of displaying the rounded ends of normal fingertips, many of the holes terminated bluntly in scar-tissue lumps.

Here was evidence that the fingers had been deliberately truncated, perhaps as part of a ritual. The Bushmen of Africa and certain North American Indians once practiced a similar type of mutilation, either as a good-luck birth ritual or to appease hunting gods. It is even possible that the amputations may have been carried out to reflect a primitive but permanent kind of sign language. The deformed hands may have been intended to symbolically represent the shapes of particular kinds of beasts important to the Cro-Magnon's livelihood or even to stand for individuals' specific animal totems or nature guardians. □

The Magical Skull of Doom

Few objects have stirred as much controversy or speculation as the crystal Skull of Doom. Life-size in its dimensions and lifelike in its execution, it has defied efforts to pinpoint its place of origin, determine its method of manufacture, or explain the strange phenomena supposedly associated with it.

The skull is said to have turned up in the 1920s under an altar in the ruins of the Mayan city of Lubaantun in British Honduras (now Belize). But doubts have been raised about its being a pre-Columbian work. Although other crystal skulls from Central America exist, none matches this one for quality of workmanship or sophistication. Moreover, the crystal from which it was made seems to have come not from Central America, but from California, where rock crystal formations of the same ◊

high quality and same size occur.

Some specialists consider the skull the product of a later culture. But then how could it have been found in a Mayan ruin, they ask? Skeptics believe the skull was a plant, buried under the altar by the British explorer-archaeologist Frederick Mitchell-Hedges, so that his adopted daughter Anna Mitchell-Hedges could come across it on her birthday as she assisted him in his excavations.

Others have suggested that the skull was never in Lubaantun or that Anna was not there on the supposed discovery day. They claim Mitchell-Hedges purchased the skull from an English owner in the 1940s and manufactured the story about Anna finding it in the Lubaantun temple, perhaps as a way of gaining publicity for it and enhancing its allure. Furthermore, they label as pure invention Mitchell-Hedges's claim that the skull was "used by

the high priest of the Maya to concentrate on and will death;" that it was "the embodiment of all evil;" and that "several people who have cynically laughed at it have died" or "have been stricken and become seriously ill."

Yet as controversy continues to swirl around it, the Skull of Doom, as Mitchell-Hedges called it, remains an object of fascination. Frank Dorland, a noted art restorer who studied it closely over a six-year period, claimed that the skull sometimes changed color or filled with a cottony haze; that it produced an "elusive perfume" and

strange tinkling sounds; that images of mountains, temples, and other objects appeared within it; and that an aura once surrounded it for several minutes. Others who saw the skull when it was in Dorland's keep reported similar phenomena, as well as such physiological reactions to it as a quickening of their pulse, a tightening of their arm and leg muscles, and even a strange tugging of their eyes.

Part of the awe the skull generates in those who behold it comes from its exquisiteness. Only the detachable lower jaw reveals faint tool marks. Whoever produced the skull had to have been a master of the first order. Just polishing it would have required weeks or even years. This genius not only finished it to perfection, but fashioned it in such a way that light concentrates in the eye sockets, providing an otherworldly glow. □

Las Bolas Grandes of Costa Rica

Even with today's tools and techniques, crafting a flawless sphere from stone by hand is a remarkably difficult challenge. And yet near-perfection in that pursuit was achieved perhaps 1,600 years ago in Central America by the carvers of Las Bolas Grandes, "the Great Stone Balls."

Ranging in diameter from eight feet to only a few inches and weighing as much as sixteen tons, the globes fairly litter the landscape of the Diquis River delta of southern Costa Rica. At least 186 of them survive whole and probably hundreds more lie buried, awaiting discovery; hundreds of others have already been irrevocably lost—through bulldozers clearing land, exposure to the elements, and native Costa Ricans who smashed the spheres in the belief that they concealed gold.

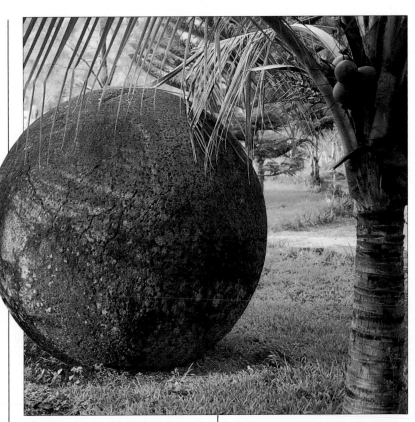

Brought to the attention of science in the 1930s when jungle was cleared for banana plantations, the spheres have undergone rigorous analysis. It is thought that the artisans who produced the stone balls used wooden templates as a means of guiding their efforts. Since almost all the spheres were made from an especially hard granite, shaping them demanded an enormous amount of patience. The process probably involved shaping the stone into a rough ball before smoothing its surface with an abrasive, perhaps sand.

However primitive their methods may have been, the artisans succeeded in turning out almost perfectly proportioned spheres. Indeed, a writer who has closely studied Las Bolas Grandes has characterized them as "perhaps the finest examples of precision stone carving in the ancient world." One sphere, measuring approximately six and a half feet in diameter, deviates in its circumference by only half an inch—or about two-tenths of one percent.

Who carved the balls and why are questions that may go forever unanswered. It is not even possible to date them effectively, since they occur in association with artifacts that span several pre-Columbian cultures. Theories as to their use range from grave markers to a form of money. A mystery too is where the Indians got the granite that they used; the nearest source lies many miles away and shows no signs of quarrying. □

The Puzzling Lines of Life

Among the oldest and most fundamental of all man-made designs are the spirals, concentric circles, and complex labyrinths with which ancient peoples decorated a variety of objects large and small.

These patterns turn up on everything from Sumerian seals, Babylonian clay tablets, and Cretan coins to Etruscan wine jugs, Roman mosaic floors, and a pillar in the ash-buried city of Pompeii. They are particularly numerous in northern Europe, where in the form of carvings they cover rocks, megaliths, and burial monuments, including one of the world's oldest surviving structures, Ireland's 5,000-year-old Newgrange tomb *(pages 86-87)*. They occur also in the New World and in Asia. Clearly, they had a hold on the ancients' psyche.

Their meaning, though, remains obscure. Some scholars have claimed that they seem to have been created less to please the eye than to jog the brain. Indeed, in whatever culture they are found, spirals and labyrinths frequently share one perplexing element; they have indirect paths leading to—or from—the center.

Scholars have spared no effort

These Cretan coins are embellished with labyrinth designs; a similar motif marks a large rock from the British Isles.

The Earth Artists

to unlock their hidden significance. One offers 104 different theories purportedly explaining them. Among the more likely explanations of spirals is that they were symbols of fertility, a metaphor for the female uterus and the process of procreation, or that they represented the bowels of the earth or perhaps the very caves in which the earliest humans worshiped and sometimes lived. In some instances, they may even have been primitive astronomical instruments with which ancient priests studied the equinoxes, the solstices, and the movements of the moon, hoping to gain mastery over the elements.

The more elaborate labyrinths are thought to represent both burial and spiritual rebirth or perhaps hypothetical maps of the underworld. Basically puzzles to which there is only one solution, labyrinths may also have illustrated the notion of exclusivity. Those who knew a labyrinth's secret could follow a direct route to or from the center. For the uninitiated, this was not so easy, many a wrong turn being made before reaching the goal. Consequently, labyrinths were to become linked in later days with Christianity, their circuitous lines portraying the difficult and often frustrating path to righteousness or heaven that devout individuals hoped to take on their journey through life. □

Some of the most remarkable monuments ever created are those drawn directly on the earth or sculpted from it by ancient peoples. These works include huge animal-shaped mounds, mystifying lines, geometric or anthropomorphic designs, and colossal figures, including the two-thousand-year-old, 393-foot Atacama Giant, scraped into a mountainside in Chile. Indeed, many of these macroforms or earthworks are so grandiose in scale that they can be seen whole only from the air or from a great distance away.

Enigmatic vestiges of cultures swallowed up by time, they occur both in the New World and the Old. Earthworks are particularly prevalent in England, the American West, and South America.

The best known perhaps are the so-called Nazca Lines of Peru, stylized drawings of monkeys, birds, lizards, spiders, flowers, and geometric shapes that range from 100 feet to five miles in length. Stretching across arid reaches of the Atacama Desert, they were made more than 1,500 years ago by Indian artists who removed the darker covering of weathered stones in order to reveal the lighter surface underneath.

The fame of the Nazca Lines has tended to overshadow other equally impressive earthworks in Chile. Here loom 300-foot-long warriors, among them the Atacama Giant, as well as llamas, spirals, circles, condors, a flying man, and a curious candelabra-like shape.

Various theories have been put forth to explain the South American earthworks. The most fanciful is that they were made not by Indians at all, but by extraterrestrials who laid them out as spaceship landing sites. Far more likely is the theory that they had magical significance for their creators, perhaps related to the mysteries of the hunt or fertility. Some scholars think that they may have served as sacred paths linking shrines, as astronomical aids, or even as a kind of colossal calendar.

There are many less-known but equally impressive earthworks in the United States, particularly in desert areas of the Southwest. More than 270 have been found along the 160-mile stretch between Bull Head City and Yuma, Arizona, and their number continues to grow as new ones are discovered in remote parts of the desert. Often using the same stone-clearing technique as their South American counterparts or aligning rocks into patterns, the North American Indians shaped huge humans, serpents, mountain lions, and other animals, as well as abstract designs. One serpentine earthwork that may be more than 5,000 years old meanders for a mile and a quarter across southeastern California.

By evaluating such physical evidence as tools found at the various sites and the physical aging of the rocks themselves, Jay von Werlhof, an archaeologist, has estimated some of the earthworks to be 10,000 years old. For clues to their meaning, he interviewed local Indians to whom the drawings continue to be sacred. His investigations suggest that they may have been created by shamans or medicine ◊

Shown here against a background of the Marching Bear mounds in McGregor, Iowa, are (clockwise from top left): the Fisherman geoglyph near Parker, Arizona; the Long Man of Wilmington chalk form in East Sussex, England; a serpentine dance pattern northeast of El Centro, California; the Rock Eagle effigy mound near Eatonton, Georgia; and the Atacama Giant on Sierra Unica Mountain in northern Chile.

men for the protection of the tribe or as a means of attracting the attention of the gods and getting them to intercede on the tribe's behalf in times of crisis. It is even thought that the Indians may have walked or danced along the lines formed by the figures as a means of absorbing the essence of whatever animal or symbol the earth artists had portrayed.

Earthworks are by no means limited to the American Southwest; they occur in the Midwest and South as well. Lacking the desert for a canvas, the earth artists in these other regions took to building effigy mounds in the shape of turtles, panthers, birds, bears, and other creatures. One of the most spectacular of these creations is the Great Serpent Mound near Chillicothe, Ohio. Constructed by the so-called Adena people, whose culture flourished between 1000 BC and AD 200, the snake coils over the landscape for nearly a quarter of a mile. At Eatonton, Georgia, rocks blanket a mound fifty centuries old that rises 10 feet from its surroundings to form an eagle 102 feet long, with a 120-foot wingspan. And at McGregor, Iowa, ten bears march one behind the other, each 3 feet high and from 80 to 100 feet long. Although only 25 other effigy mounds survive in Iowa today, the state once had 375 of them.

In England, earthworks of another sort dominate the landscape. On the green slopes of the chalk downs of southern England, some fifty earthworks were made by artists who cut through the turf to reveal the white strata underneath. The most impressive is the Long Man of Wilmington in East Sussex, second only to the Atacama Giant in scale. Carved into a hillside, the figure stands 231 feet tall, with square shoulders 46 feet broad, a waist 23 feet wide, and legs 100 feet long—each limb as wide as a country lane. No one knows precisely how old the Wilmington giant is; but there is speculation that it may date back 2,500 years.

A similar giant, this one boldly naked and wielding a club, measures 180 feet and overlooks the Dorset village of Cerne Abbas. But experts widely disagree on its age: Some say it dates to 2,000 years ago, while others maintain that it is only about 300 years old. □

China's See-Through Mirrors

For centuries, people have been amazed by the solid metal "magic mirrors" of China. When held up to light, the mirrors seem to allow the light to pass through, projecting the image of raised decorations on the back onto a white wall. Yet the image does not show on the mirror's face.

Dating from the Western Han period of 206 BC to AD 9, these mirrors and their decorations were cast from bronze and their slightly convex faces made very thin by careful grinding, scraping, and polishing. The mirrors baffled generations of Chinese after the secret of their manufacture seemed to die with their creators. One eleventh-century scholar, who had three of these so-called light-penetration mirrors, pondered their mystery in an essay but could not understand "why other mirrors, though extremely thin, do not let light through."

The magic mirrors caused a considerable stir when they finally came to the attention of Westerners in 1832. Some of the best scientific minds of the day tried to figure out how they worked, but the investigators wound up being as stymied as the Chinese had been. A century would pass before the mystery was solved.

The secret lay on the face. There, casting and polishing had produced slight variations—invisible to the naked eye—that corresponded to the raised designs on the back. When light struck this irregular surface, it bounced off all the many minute ups and downs, reproducing the decoration as a magnified reflection. □

This intriguing Chinese "magic mirror" (left) is from the first century BC. Above, the mirror's image is reflected onto a flat surface.

The Under-ground Army

China's first true emperor, Qin Shi Huangdi—who ruled from 221 to 206 BC—willed into existence wonders the likes of which the ancient world had never seen before. Not only did he order much of the Great Wall of China built, he also had monuments glorifying himself produced on such a scale that they bedazzle the mind to this day.

Not content with one palace, he erected 270 of them in his capital, Xianyang. Seven hundred thousand convict laborers worked on his primary residence alone; its vast terraces were spacious enough to have held 10,000 subjects at a time. His mausoleum, begun when he was only thirteen years old, was executed on a similar scale and became part of a complex measuring nearly four square miles. In the words of a historian writing a century after its completion, the tomb was "fitted with models of palaces, pavilions and offices, as well as fine vessels, precious stones and rarities." Even more miraculous, "all the country's streams, the Yellow River, and the Yangtze were reproduced in quicksilver, and by some mechanical means made to flow into a miniature ocean."

Although Qin Shi Huangdi's palaces have long since moldered into dust, his mausoleum survives under a 150-foot mound of earth. One day it will be explored, but in the meantime, archaeologists with an interest in the site have much else to occupy their time.

In 1974, well diggers working in the vicinity of the burial mound found bits and pieces of statues representing humans and horses—and set off one of the most stunning excavations of modern time. As archaeologists carefully troweled away the earth in what proved to be an enormous pit, they began laying bare the first traces of an entire army—life-size figures of terra-cotta warriors and horses.

Subsequent test digs in the surrounding area revealed two other pits with more soldiers buried in them. All three pits had once been roofed over and covered with dirt to conceal the underground force that symbolically guarded the mausoleum.

Work concentrated on the first pit, in which more than 1,000 figures have since come to light, with an estimated 5,000 others yet to be ⟩

excavated. Three rows of 70 fierce-looking warriors stand in the foreground. Behind the rows of warriors stretch thirty-eight columns of infantrymen divided into eleven groups. The clay figures are dressed in armor, and in their hands they once held spears, swords, and crossbows. The metal weapons, which fell to the ground when the wooden handles rotted away, remain as sharp and shiny as on the day that the figures were consigned to darkness.

Only preliminary work has been carried out on the other two pits, but it is enough to suggest that they hold military treasure of their own. The second pit is believed to contain another 1,000 soldiers, plus 80 chariots drawn by 400 horses. The third pit, with far fewer figures, may represent headquarters for the guardian army.

The miracle of this clay army is not just its size, but the quality of its execution and the minute attention to detail given it by the anonymous sculptors. The uniforms and headgear vary by rank and were originally brightly painted. Down to the shape of a mustache or the cold stare of an obvious veteran, each face is unique, suggesting that the figures were modeled on actual soldiers.

The production of such imposing statues—the warriors stand six feet tall—required great technical skill. Even today, creating such figures would take tremendous effort, with a framework of metal or wood necessary to support them and keep them from becoming distorted during firing. Although the work on the site will go on for years, the emperor's army is already known as the Eighth Wonder of the Ancient World. □

A Race of Stone Giants

Few places in the world are as remote as Easter Island. Yet somehow, men, women, and children of the fourth century AD found their way from Polynesia to this 69-square-mile dot in the Pacific, 2,300 miles west of Chile and 1,300 miles east of Pitcairn Island, and established a culture remarkable for its achievements. Not only did the Easter Islanders evolve a form of writing uniquely their own, develop a sophisticated system of solar observation, and bring rock and cave painting to a high art; they also produced over a 900-year-period the estimated 1,000 stone heads, or *moai*, for which the island has become so famous.

Carved out of soft, yellowish volcanic rock and crowned with huge cylindrical topknots of red stone, the finished moai faced inland on massive altars, called *ahu*, that marked the burial sites of kings, chiefs, and other important personages. Early European voyagers, who first encountered the island in the eighteenth century, saw hundreds of the stone heads standing along the coastline. Yet the number of statues was once far greater. Either for unknown religious reasons, a shift in belief, or because of growing competition and aggressiveness among the various groups of moai builders, many of the giants had already been toppled. And by the mid-nineteenth century, the rest of the statues had been sent crashing to the ground.

Today, nearly thirty of the monoliths once again stand upright, put back in place by archaeologists. The rest lie where they fell or were left unfinished. The vertical ones rear twelve to twenty-five feet high. Of the fallen monoliths, the largest, measuring thirty-two feet long and weighing 80 tons, had to be transported five miles from the quarry to its present site, then raised and crowned with a 12-ton stone top-knot. What would have been the biggest statue of all is still attached to the volcanic rock from which it was being cut; it is sixty-nine feet long and is estimated to weigh about 270 tons. Had it been erected, it would have loomed as high as a six-story building.

Confronted by the awesome dimensions of the stone giants, explorers at first doubted that the Easter Islanders could have carved them with the primitive stone tools at their disposal, much less have moved the statues from the quarry to the distant sites they occupy. In the years since, some enthusiasts have sought to explain the heads as the work of a lost civilization, perhaps Atlantis *(pages 130-131)*—or even of inter-planetary visitors.

Several more mundane theories have been put forth to explain how the Easter Islanders raised their statues. The most likely explanation is that once the carvers freed a figure from the stone, they placed it on a sledge, face down, and inched it along with the aid of a wooden device—attached by ropes to the neck—that lifted the head and thrust it forward. The islanders then raised the statue by piling rocks under it and levered it into an upright position with the aid of logs.

As the quest for power and prestige grew among the islanders, the need to erect ever bigger statues apparently accelerated. Those groups with the most imposing moai doubtless had control over many of the island's resources, particularly its agriculture. But as the population grew, reaching a peak of perhaps 15,000, resources began to fail. Once densely forest-ed, the island was all but stripped bare of its trees as more and more land was turned over to farming. Deprived of wood, the islanders lost the means to transport and raise their statues, as well as the opportunity to build ocean-going canoes that might have enabled them to emigrate elsewhere as crowding grew intolerable.

When Peruvian slavers captured 2,000 of the inhabitants between 1859 and 1862, including the king, his son, and numerous priests, and took them to South America, the Easter Islanders and their culture were dealt a blow from which they would never recover. The eventual return of a few who survived their South American servitude spread diseases for which the remaining inhabitants had no resistance. By 1877, the once-proud Easter Islanders had dwindled to no more than 150, and with the eventual deaths of these—the last holders of the ancient traditions—the secrets of the moai went to the grave. □

The Enigma of Scotland's Stone Balls

Perfectly carved stone balls at least thirty centuries old have been turning up for years in Scotland, tantalizing scholars with the mystery of their origin and function. To date, well over 350 balls have been discovered, mostly between the towns of Aberdeenshire and Angus.

Measuring from one inch to three and a half inches in diameter, some are incised with spirals, concentric circles, and other geometric designs; some are unadorned; some have knobs. Few show hard wear, but several are conspicuously smooth, suggesting that they were much valued and often handled.

All sorts of theories have been put forth to explain these ancient spheres. They were at first thought to be weapons, perhaps lashed to handles with leather thongs, like maces, or tied to the ends of thongs and used as bolas. But the grooves cut in them are too shallow for thongs to have been attached securely. Another theory suggested that the balls may have been used in some type of competitive game. However, few of them show any extensive damage. Indeed, the smoothness of so many has led some researchers to conclude that the balls may have been portable symbols of power, not unlike coats of arms. Since they are relatively small and fairly light in weight, they may have been carried by leaders in leather pouches worn at the waist and passed down from generation to generation. If so, this would explain why the balls have never been discovered in any graves. □

SKY WATCHERS

Scanning the heavens with high-technology telescopes and spacecraft, modern astronomers have fashioned an understanding of the universe far beyond what was thought possible only a few decades ago. Yet, in a sense, the achievements of these scientists are less remarkable than those of ancient sky watchers—the priests, shamans, and philosophers of long-vanished societies. Somehow, through observation, intuition, and methods now lost in time, these scholars amassed a wealth of knowledge about the movements of the sun, moon, planets, and stars and how they might be linked to the rhythms of humankind, of sowing and reaping, life and death.

History does not say when or why humans first began noting and recording patterns of motion among celestial bodies. Certainly they were driven partly by an early realization that time was a dimension of life and that, in the apparent chaos of a primitive world, there was order to be found among the stars.

Whatever their motives, it appears that—in nearly every region of the world and with tools and techniques of their own devising—the ancients reached a sophisticated understanding of a number of complex celestial phenomena a long time before the beginning of the historical record. Some of them may have learned how to predict eclipses; others may even have grasped the notion that the earth is not flat, but round.

Since the 1960s, a new branch of scholarship called archaeoastronomy has emerged to trace the full extent of this considerable ancient knowledge. By studying the artifacts and lore of early human communities, archaeoastronomers hope to discover how these societies learned about the heavens and how and why they used their insights in agriculture, philosophy, and religion. But the researchers are dogged by a frustrating certainty: Much of what they seek has been lost beyond retrieving. The astronomers of old will keep many of their secrets through eternity.

A Sunbeam for the Dead

Thirty miles north of Dublin stands one of the great astronomical wonders of prehistoric Europe. On a long, low ridge overlooking the narrow Boyne River, ancient farmers built a mound more than 260 feet in diameter and 30 feet high. Its southern edge, facing the river, is banded with a wall of sparkling white quartz. At the middle of this wall, guarded by a massive, intricately carved stone, is an entryway: For the mound is more than a heap of stones; it is a shell enclosing an early masterpiece of megalithic architecture.

The entrance opens onto a passage sixty-two feet long, a buried avenue flanked by forty-three stones—most of them taller than a man and weighing ten to twelve tons each. At the end of the passage lies a complex structure of huge rocks, some carved with symbolic designs, forming a cross-shaped chamber that rises into a vault some twenty feet above the floor. On the floor of each arm of the cross lies a basin stone—a large, flat rock with a shallow indentation carved into it. In this area bodies of the dead were placed, corpses now broken and scattered by time and marauding animals. The roof stones are grooved to carry water away from

the chamber, and their seams are sealed with puttylike burned soil.

Newgrange, as the structure is called, is the largest and most elaborate of a trio of New Stone Age tombs put down by early Irish farmers in this bend in the Boyne. This house of the dead predates the completion of England's Stonehenge by 1,000 years and Egypt's pyramids by several centuries. But Newgrange is more than a tomb; it appears to have been meant as a kind of cathedral to the life force embodied in the sun.

During a restoration of the mound that began in 1960, two Irish archaeologists, Michael and Claire O'Kelly, discovered a vertical opening between roof slabs above the entrance to Newgrange. Set in the gap was a decorated, open-ended structure they dubbed the roof box. In 1969, acting on a hunch, the O'Kellys stationed themselves in the tomb's interior passageway at dawn on December 21. This day marked the winter solstice, when the sun stops its retreat from the northern hemisphere and the dark winter days begin to lengthen into spring.

Four minutes after sunrise, they noted, "the first pencil of direct sunlight shone through the roof box and right along the passage to reach across the tomb chamber floor as far as the front edge of the basin stone in the end chamber. As the thin line of light widened . . . and swung across the chamber floor, the tomb was dramatically illuminated." The solar beam began to narrow; seventeen minutes after the sun appeared in the roof-box aperture, it vanished. The subterranean light show, the O'Kellys discovered, began about a week before the winter solstice and continued for a week afterward. For that short interval each year, sunlight entered Newgrange so that only the dead could see it.

Although many

As the sun reaches its southernmost point in the sky, a shaft of sunlight shoots through a narrow gap above the entrance to Newgrange, illuminating an inner burial chamber.

scholars thought it likely that this precise solar alignment was mere chance, others believed it must have been deliberate. Convincing proof of this did not come until 1988, however, when Tom P. Ray, an astrophysicist at the Dublin Institute for Advanced Studies, investigated Newgrange and found that the central passage, though slightly winding, would have been aligned with the midwinter sunrise of 5,150 years ago. It would have permitted a single beam of light to enter the chamber not four minutes after, but at the exact moment of sunrise. Obviously, the architects of the day did not achieve such close tolerances only by accident.

Ray's discovery was significant for researchers seeking to understand the Neolithic people of Ireland, who left behind nothing except such monuments. Their culture seems to have first appeared about 10,000 years ago, when human agriculture began, then vanished before the first written histories of civilization. Archaeologists now think that the workers who built the tombs were drawn from a very small population—perhaps as few as 3,000 people. The complexity, workmanship, and precision of the structure shows that this ancient society had planning and building skills far beyond what had formerly been attributed to them.

But all of these abilities, it appears, focused on tomb building, and the compulsion to celebrate the deceased bore the seeds of ruin for the living. Newgrange seems to have been the product of an intensifying obsession with death. Ultimately, the building of such tombs so depleted the wealth of the builders that their economy collapsed and the land was left to lie fallow. A thousand years after its builders' time, Newgrange was simply an overgrown mound above the Boyne, where squatters set down their sparse communities and cattle grazed, and once a year, a slender beam of sunlight brought intimations of life to the remains of the dead. □

Round Earth Roundup

Christopher Columbus's conclusion that the world is round would have come as old news to the ancients.

"The earth is a globe," said Pythagoras, the Greek philosopher of the fifth century BC. Two centuries later another Greek, Aristarchus of Samos, affirmed the earth's shape and added that it spun on its axis and, with other planets, revolved around the sun. Also in the third century BC, Eratosthenes, custodian of the library at Alexandria, used his knowledge of astronomy to measure with considerable accuracy the earth's circumference and diameter.

Ancient writings indicate that the sages of India knew of the world's spherical shape by the fourth century BC, and the Chinese even earlier than that—perhaps as long as 3,000 years ago. □

Moon among the Stones

On a ridge above Loch Roag in Scotland's Outer Hebrides, columns of rock stand like mournful giants. They are the Callanish stones, among the most remote of the hundreds of stone circles erected as early as 5,000 years ago across the British Isles and Brittany. But Callanish is something more: Of all the megalithic sites, it most powerfully evokes ancient understanding of the skies.

The pillars were emplaced about 2000 BC by the New Stone Age inhabitants of the Isle of Lewis, who arranged them in a rough Celtic cross—a cross circled by a ring—oriented toward the south (right). The design centers on a five-ton gneiss megalith more than fifteen feet high, ringed by thirteen slightly shorter companions. To the north, an avenue flanked by two lines of standing stones extends some 250 feet. A shorter single line of stones marches southward from the circle, which is intermittently surrounded by individual slabs of rock, seemingly set down at random. Closer scrutiny suggests, however, that Callanish's shape is in no way random but was shaped by a grand astronomical design.

According to most modern researchers, the Callanish stones were set up partly to mark the extreme northern and southern

points of the moon's rising and setting. In an erratic imitation of the sun's steady year-long journey between solstices—the northernmost and southernmost points in

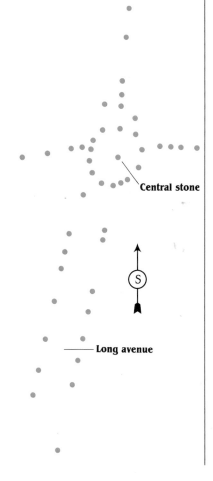

Central stone

S

Long avenue

its apparent track across the sky—the moon's path shifts slowly toward the north and south, reaching a maximum position at precise intervals of 18.61 years. Because the moon's path extends no farther north or south than these maximum points, the phenomenon is sometimes given the misleading label of "lunar standstill," although the moon continues its rapid daily crossing of the heavens.

The complex orbital variations that produce this effect were first explained by Sir Isaac Newton in the seventeenth century and later elaborated by Europe's brilliant eighteenth-century astronomers. But it now appears almost certain that this lengthy lunar cycle—so long that even the long-lived humans of today must stretch to experience four of them in a lifetime—was known to a Neolithic race whose average life span would scarcely permit cognizance of more than one cycle.

Callanish was apparently designed to reveal this dazzling lunar vision, which can be seen only at far northern latitudes in midwinter and midsummer—and only for a short interval every eighteen and a half years. One alignment of stones radiating from the center of the cross, for example, denotes a point on the far southwestern horizon where the midsummer moon sets

Every 18.61 years, the midsummer full moon rises and sets almost due south of Callanish, barely grazing the southern horizon on its short track across the sky (top). Evidently, the stones were arranged (above) to mark this setting of the moon.

during one such extreme. Then, the full moon in its passage across the sky barely grazes the crests of the hills to the south across the loch, vanishing, reappearing, then vanishing once again. Seen from the long avenue, this horizon-skimming moon moves through the ranked megaliths like a shining spirit, alternately hidden and revealed by the columns.

Seeing the moon among those pillars set one modern observer on a lifelong quest to decipher the stones. In 1934, Alexander Thom, an engineering professor at Oxford University and an ardent sailor, steered his small sailboat into Loch Roag, where he saw on the ridge above a tableau that would alter his life: the stones of Callanish silhouetted against the disk of the moon rising to the east. He hurried ashore and approached the columns, noticing as he did that the short line of standing rocks above the horizontal member of the cross aimed directly at the north star—the center of the sky's apparent rotation. The eerie moonrise and the seemingly deliberate orientation of the stones moved him deeply. "From that minute," Thom wrote later, "I knew I had to deal with a highly developed culture, and everything I have uncovered since lends support to that."

Although Thom was among the first to conclude that Callanish was built to show the lunar standstill, he was not the first to attribute astronomical precision to such monuments; others had made that connection more than two centuries earlier. But he was the most determined. After critics derided his astronomical case for Callanish, Thom devoted much of his spare time to quantifying what he had witnessed there. With his engineer son, Archibald, Thom tramped the remote reaches of the British Isles, making careful surveys of megalithic monuments and interpreting their alignments in astronomical terms.

Decades of study led him to conclude that the megaliths' builders had been far more than primitive farmers. To mark the lunar standstills, they must have been capable of systematic observation over generations. Although Thom's view has its detractors, it may explain why the Callanish megaliths are arranged the way they are.

But it does not explain why Stone Age farmers spent years cutting, transporting, and erecting such huge and heavy slabs of rock. Working at Stonehenge in the early 1960s, Gerald Hawkins, a British-born astronomer then lecturing at Boston University, concluded that such megalithic sites were designed as rudimentary comput-

ers, used to predict two of the most fearsomely portentous of heavenly events: solar and lunar eclipses. Hawkins's theory was echoed and extended by Thom, who interpreted Callanish and many other stone rings and cruciforms as the work of Neolithic scientists capable of such predictions.

Indeed, the sun, moon, and earth are aligned during the extreme lunar standstill, so that the 18.61-year lunar cycle coincides with what modern astronomers call eclipse seasons—periods when eclipses are likely to occur. The ponderous computer would have invested early leaders with the power to predict intervals when these events—dreaded by the ancients as signs of impending doom—might occur. The brooding stones may have been a kind of early warning system against those fearsome nights when darkness would swallow the full moon over the moor at Callanish. □

Oenopides of Chios, a Greek philosopher of the fifth century BC, is credited with being the first to calculate the angle of the earth's tilt on its axis. He computed the slant at 24 degrees with respect to the plane of earth's orbit, only .5 degrees from the currently accepted angle of 23.5 degrees.

Astronomy of the Unseen

Sirius, the primary star in the constellation Canis Majoris, is the brightest in earth's sky. Known as the Dog Star, it has long figured in human cosmology and myth. In 1836, German astronomer Friedrich Bessel discovered that something tugging at Sirius caused an almost imperceptible wobble in the star's orbit. Apparently, the Dog Star was circled by a fainter star every fifty years.

The unseen companion, labeled Sirius B, was not viewed until 1862, when an American telescope-maker named Alvan Clark saw it through his 18.5-inch refractor, then the world's most powerful telescope. More than half a century later, astronomers at California's Mount Wilson Observatory established that Sirius B was a new type of super-dense star they called a white dwarf: a stellar left-over that had collapsed into a ball of highly compressed material.

But the most puzzling aspect of Sirius B was announced in 1950, not by astronomers but by two distinguished French anthropologists just back from what is now the Republic of Mali. According to Marcel Griaule and Germaine Dieterlen, the white dwarf, though quite invisible to the naked eye, had been the celestial keystone of an African tribe's cosmology for centuries.

Griaule and Dieterlen had gone to live with the Dogon tribe in its sub-Saharan corner of French

Sudan in 1931. By 1946, the tribe had come to trust Griaule enough to reveal their cosmology to him. As the Frenchman watched, Dogon holy men and women used sticks to scratch a rough oval diagram of the heavens in the dirt. Before long, Griaule could make out in the drawing the Dog Star, and around it, in elliptical orbit, a companion star, along with another unseen body that has not yet been detected by astronomers. According to the Dogon, the egg-shaped orbit represented fertility: the "egg of the world." The companion star circled Sirius A in a period of fifty years, they explained, and was so small that they named it *po* for their tiniest

seed, a grain called *digitaria exilis*.

Digitaria, as Griaule labeled the companion star, was said to be made of a metal the Dogon called *sagala*, brighter than iron and so heavy that "all earthly beings combined cannot lift it."

Griaule found that the verisimilitude of the Dogon cosmos goes well beyond Sirius. They rightly believe, for example, that Jupiter has four large moons, Saturn is ringed, the earth revolves around the sun, and stars spin, as they do in the real universe.

How could tribal myth that predated telescopes have come so close to astronomical reality? Some researchers treat the celestial knowledge of the Dogon as an enigma that can only be resolved by invoking extraordinary and improbable means such as divination or psychic viewing. Others, though, note that the Dogon are neither as primitive nor as isolated as certain reports have made them out to be. Their villages of tightly clustered mud huts lie along overland trade routes that once linked West Africa with ancient Egypt and border the Niger River, a major regional conduit of commerce. They live just south of Timbuktu, the seat of a university that, 400 years ago, was one of Islam's great intellectual centers. And the Dogon have been able to attend French schools in the area since 1907. All these factors lead many scholars to attribute the tribe's knowledge of the skies to cultural interchange, transfers among various cultures— or even outright fraud.

Cultural interactions may well explain some of the details of their cosmology. But the congruence between the real Sirius star system and the mythic one constructed by the Dogon continues to bemuse investigators.

To the tribe, however, there is no mystery. Many years ago, they say, amphibious beings called *nommo* from the Sirius star system brought the Dogon special knowledge of the heavens, then returned home. With very few exceptions, only the Dogon believe this. But no one else has quite explained how, in their rough celestial diagrams, the Africans can describe stars they have still not seen. □

A Cryptic Disk

One evening in 1971, wealthy amateur philologist Leon Pomerance looked up at a simulation of the star-strewn sky of ancient Crete. With him was Kenneth Franklin, an astronomer who in 1955 had shared in the discovery of the planet Jupiter's radio emissions and who now worked at the American Museum's Hayden Planetarium in New York. For this occasion, Franklin had programmed the planetarium's projector to display the star patterns that would have appeared 4,000 years ago. Pomerance had noted this sequence of constellations before but not on a conventional star chart. Rather, he had discerned the peculiar lineup of stars on the weathered face of one of prehistory's most inscrutable objects: the Phaistos Disk.

Discovered in 1908 by Italian archaeologist Luigi Pernier, the disk was part of a trove dug from ruins of the city-palace of Phaistos, a center of the Minoan civilization that thrived in Crete from about 3000 to 1100 BC. The Phaistos Disk is a terra-cotta plate six inches across, marked with some forty-five different pictograms of people, animals, and designs, repeated in various combinations along a spiral band that coils to an end in the plate's center.

The disk's symbols—among them dot clusters, a bird, a bear, a serpentine squiggle, and a profiled human head—are completely unlike those of Linear A and Linear B, the known hieroglyphic systems ◊

and the cluster of the Pleiades, which seemed to correspond to a serpent's tail, a soaring bird, and a dotted circle on the Phaistos Disk. A fourth symbol, a head emitting rays, he took to be the sun. Pomerance guessed that the disk was the work of ancient astronomers who had painstakingly observed and recorded the transit of these bodies through the skies.

Putting his theory to the test, Pomerance enlisted the aid of Kenneth Franklin at the Hayden Planetarium. There, beneath the recreated Cretan heavens of 2000 BC, Franklin ordered the computer to set the ancient sky in motion, and the men watched the constellations move swiftly through their seasonal changes. First Serpens Cauda, the

of the Minoans. Moreover, while scripts of Linear A and B were usually incised with a writing instrument, the Phaistos glyphs appear to have been pressed into the clay with small dies—a kind of prehistoric analogue to movable type.

For some experts, the disk's puzzle is purely linguistic. But their efforts at translation have been inconclusive. For example, markings one scholar translated as "the predatory bird flies over the threshing floor in the town" another read as "from the sacrificial drink." Steven Fischer, a West German linguist, developed a poetic translation of both sides of the disk in 1984. One side was a call to arms against the neighboring Carians; the obverse, said Fischer, was a prayer for protection from enemies. Still other linguists, noting

the disk's scanty vocabulary, maintain that the ancient markings will never be translated.

Leon Pomerance, however, saw the Phaistos enigma differently. The symbols, he believed, were graphics; like the glyphs on modern road signs, they represented things, not sounds. Then, looking at star map, he saw the constellations Serpens Cauda, Aquila,

Serpent's Tail, emerged in what would have been late November, followed by Aquila, the Eagle, which seemed to fly toward the west. As the simulation progressed, the seven-star Pleiades rose in April, just before the sun. The year unfolded, and the stars made their turnings: By October, the Eagle had reversed itself and flew eastward, upside down. Pomerance had seen this sequence before, pressed into the surface of the Phaistos Disk. The mysterious plate, he concluded, was a kind of early almanac, probably used by farmers to chronicle planting and harvesting.

This interpretation won cautious endorsement from some authorities, but there is no consensus. Today, what may be one of the first human records of seasonal changes in the sky waits in the Heraklion Museum on Crete for confirmation, perhaps by a companion object dredged from the Aegean or discovered within Minoan ruins. □

An Ancient Computer

For 2,000 years, the wreckage of a Greek merchant ship lay undisturbed beneath the gale-swept waters of the eastern Mediterranean, its ghostly hulk shrouded in silt. Littering the seafloor along its 150-foot length were relics of its riches: storage jars, statuary, unidentifiable bits and oddments consigned to the deep. Then, in 1900, sponge fishermen diving for their catch in a bay off a barren islet called Antikythera chanced on the ship's wreckage—and transformed forever modern notions about ancient Greece.

The Antikythera find was archaeology's first great underwater discovery, and as such it caused a great stir in scholarly circles. Artifacts from the ancient wreck made their way to the Greek National Archaeological Museum in Athens, where they were scrutinized, catalogued, and assembled. Smaller pieces were set aside as possible missing parts. Among these were four heavily corroded lumps of bronze, which were examined by museum archaeologist Valerios Staïs. He noticed that what had at first appeared to be simply scratches on the metal were in fact an inscription. Looking more closely, he saw that the bronze fragments were actually clusters of geared wheels—the remnant of some kind of machine.

Further study of the pieces led Staïs to conclude in 1902 that the device dated from the first century BC and that it appeared to be a navigational tool, perhaps an early astrolabe, an instrument used to determine the positions of celestial bodies. There speculation

about the artifact stood until 1951, when Professor Derek de Solla Price of Yale University began what would become the definitive study of the Antikythera Mechanism, as it had come to be called. Attempting to re-create the device, Price and his Greek co-workers used x-rays and gamma-rays to probe the internal structure. The mechanism, he discovered, contained layer upon layer of varioussized gears. After long calculations of possible gear ratios, Price arrived at an astonishing conclusion: Some ancient Greek inventor had designed a mechanism that mimicked the actual movements of the sun, moon, and planets, past, present, and future. The Antikythera Mechanism was a 2,000-yearold analog computer.

As hypothetically reconstructed by Price, the original mechanism consisted of a rectangular box about twelve by six by three inches, with the bronze machinery contained by wooden sides. The front and back were covered by bronze doors on which the inventor had inscribed detailed instructions. Three dials displayed the device's "readout." The first contained two concentric bands, one showing the signs of the zodiac, a sixteen-degree-wide belt straddling the apparent path of the sun, and the other the names of the Greek months. A pointer revealed the position of the sun in the zodiac for every day of the year. A second dial displayed an eighteen-year cycle of solar eclipses, while a third kept track of the different phases of the moon.

Inside the box, some thirty- ◊

In this schematic re-creation of the Cretan sky in about 2000 BC, rising constellations mimic the order of symbols on the Phaistos Disk. On the eastern horizon *(rear)*, the Serpent's Tail rises in late November; followed in December by the Eagle *(center)*; and, in the spring, by the Pleiades *(front)*.

same principle that allows the traction wheels on modern automobiles to turn at different rates on curves, the differential gear had long been assumed to be an invention of the seventeenth century.

Fascinated by Price's hypothesis, physicist Allan Bromley, a professor at the University of Sydney, enlisted the help of clockmaker Frank Percival to construct a working model of the Antikythera Mechanism. Using techniques that would have been available to the ancient Greeks, in 1987 the pair assembled a functional replica that largely verified a majority of Price's theories.

Still, the identity of the machine's original creator is lost in time. Some scholars believe that the Antikythera Mechanism originated on the island of Rhodes, where cultural conditions two thousand years ago might have been right for the emergence of the necessary skills. There, without any fanfare, a consummate mechanical artisan who had a strong knowledge of the heavens somehow fashioned the ancient computer of Antikythera, the device that Price called one of "the greatest basic mechanical inventions of all time."

Rising from its watery grave after two millennia, the mechanism belied the prevailing view that ancient Greece was a land of brilliant theoreticians who, pampered by slaves, disdained the physical. These Greeks, it seems, had a mechanical genius after all. □

nine bronze gears were meshed on parallel planes and set in motion by a handle that needed to be turned once a day. These were linked through a kind of toothed turntable that acted as a differential gear train, permitting two shafts to rotate at different speeds. Operating on the

Sun Stones

Gazing through smoky crystal or translucent jade, Chinese astronomers observed sunspots—black blotches caused by relatively cool areas in the sun's atmosphere—at least 1,600 years before the Italian astronomer Galileo saw them through his telescope.

Many ancient Chinese histories and memoirs refer to sunspots, and historians believe that observ-

ing the sun through the filters of semitransparent stones was an early Chinese practice. Some scholars theorize that haze from dust storms in the Gobi also provided Chinese astronomers with a natural filter for solar study. □

The Crescent and the Star

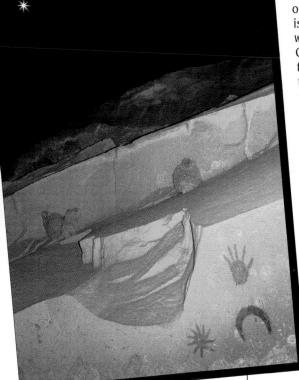

A photographic re-creation of the Crab supernova near the crescent moon before sunrise on July 5, 1054, simulates the sky as seen by the Anasazi pictogram artist from Chaco Canyon.

The now-vanished civilization of the Anasazi Indians flourished in the American Southwest about 1,000 years ago. On the baked plateaus of the high desert, ruins of their stone cities and mysterious roadways *(page 69)* offer mute witness to Anasazi craft and tenacity. And the rocky, earth-hued mesas hint at another of their talents: astronomy.

Modern archaeoastronomers interpret certain signs on the desert rocks to mean that the Anasazi were systematic sky watchers who understood much about the heavens. On a ledge near the top of a towering butte *(above)* in New Mexico's Chaco Canyon, for instance, three large sandstone slabs formed an aperture through which sunlight played in enigmatic ways along two spirals carved in the rock face behind the stones. For perhaps 1,000 years, until the late 1980s when erosion

caused the slabs to shift, shafts of light accurately demarked the summer and winter solstices—the longest and shortest days of the year—as well as the March and September equinoxes, the times when day and night are of equal length. Scholars believe that the Sun Dagger, as the phenomenon has come to be called, was a calendar devised by the Anasazi.

Testament to the astronomical acumen of the Anasazi does not, however, rest with the Sun Dagger alone: Chaco Canyon's stones also hint that these sky watchers saw and chronicled the death of a star.

On a cliff beneath the ruins of an Anasazi town called Penasco Blanco, an overhanging rock bears on its underside three painted designs: a crescent, a rayed disk, and a hand. Directly below them on the sandstone wall is painted a dot circled by two rings, still recognized by modern Pueblo Indians as the sign for the sun.

Found in 1972 by archaeologists from the University of New Mexico, the symbols, which appear to mark the post of the former Anasazi sun watchers, echo markings found ◊

at other such posts in the southwestern Indian territories. To some astronomers, the symbols evoke nothing more remarkable than the occasional proximity of Venus and the moon. But, because the crescent is relatively rare in southwestern rock art, several experts believe that the painted objects—those at Chaco Canyon especially—must commemorate a spectacular celestial event. The rayed disk, they speculate, might denote an exploding star. The Chaco Canyon images were painted during the most active era of Anasazi civilization, about a millennium ago. At that time, across the world in China, astronomers reported the appearance of a "guest star," probably the bright explosion, or supernova, marking the death of exceptionally massive stars. According to the Chinese, the guest star appeared on July 5, 1054, a day when the predawn sky blazed with a new object five or six times brighter than Venus—the brightest star besides the sun ever seen by humans. Its remnants are the Crab nebula, a vast and still-expanding cloud of gas in the constellation Taurus.

Might the Chaco Canyon pictograms record that same titanic explosion? Some researchers think they must. Hoping to verify it, NASA astronomer John Brandt, in 1979, asked a colleague at the U.S. Naval Observatory in Washington, D.C., to reproduce the southwestern night sky as it would have been in July 1054. In those long-ago heavens, the astronomers discovered, the moon, an inverted crescent, was barely two degrees (about four lunar diameters) away from the Crab nebula, almost exactly as shown on the rock at Chaco Canyon.

If this evidence can be trusted, nearly 1,000 years ago an Anasazi sun watcher took up his post on the cliff below Penasco Blanco just before sunrise. As he watched the eastern horizon, the moon rose with a star of astonishing brilliance suspended almost in the curve of its upside-down crescent. Fascinated by the bright stranger in the skies, the observer commemorated its appearance with an indelible portrait in rock. □

ANCIENTS AT PLAY

Play is as old as the human race. It is, in fact, the rehearsal children need to become full-fledged adults. Of course, play does not vanish with childhood but persists into adulthood as an exhilarating celebration of life. What is surprising, perhaps, is that the ancients were greatly like us in this. They enjoyed cards, dice, and board games and had their athletic contests and spectator sports, with audiences numbering in the thousands.

To the Greeks, play was basic to survival. Being able to hurl a spear or stone with force or defend one's self in combat was the mark of a good citizen, and there was only one way for a man to achieve such prowess—through athletics. The Greeks believed that in competing they were honoring the gods. It was no accident, then, that they founded the Olympic Games and kept the event going for more than eleven centuries, until the Christian emperor Theodosius I finally closed the games in AD 393.

But if Greek play was essentially a healthy expression of mind and of body, the play of others in the ancient world could be colored by violent urges. The Romans developed a taste for gore, pitting people and beasts or gladiator and gladiator against each other in battles to the death. Gladiators, the sports heroes of the day, fought with a regular armory at their disposal—swords, lances, barbed pikes and forks, metal nets. Boxers wore iron spikes on their fists. Across the seas, in a world yet unknown to Europeans, the Maya gave their own games a similar bloody cast; in fact, they took one ball game so seriously that the losers were decapitated as a way of placating the gods.

Deadly Child's Play

At one end of the arena stood a great bull with forbidding horns; at the other, an unarmed human waited expectantly. As the bull charged, its intended victim stood his ground without visible fear until, an instant before he would surely be impaled, he grasped the tips of the horns and vaulted over the bull, turning a somersault over the animal's back before landing on the ground behind it.

No documents survive to provide a description of this deadly pastime, practiced by the Minoans on Crete sometime during the middle of the second millennium BC. But an abundance of detailed wall decorations, showing massive bulls and diminutive humans *(below)*, have led scholars to the startling conclusion that the ancient bull leapers were not muscular adults but specially trained boys and girls who were agile and light enough to be lifted over the menacing horns.

Some historians suggest that bull leaping may have been a ritual contest, perhaps a form of fertility or coming-of-age rite. Others say it was just a sport, performed during religious festivals. Whatever the intent, it was not a blood sport, at least not in the sense of modern bullfighting. No weapons were used, and the only danger was to human beings. Indeed, some Cretan paintings show the bull-leaping acrobats being gored. □

The Golden Wreath

The spirit of peace and the love of sport for its own sake that are invoked in the modern Olympics were not always evident during the nearly twelve centuries of the ancient Olympics. In fact, these original games, held at the magnificent Greek city and sports complex of Olympia, were riddled with professionalism, bribery, chicanery, and political intrigue.

Such imperfections were rooted, perhaps, in the very word *athlete*, Greek for "prize seeker." The Greeks took this literally and provided ample rewards for their Olympic heroes. Although the official prize for winners was a wild olive wreath, victors were showered with more substantial rewards—cash, free housing, and other privileges—by their home states. Also-rans received nothing for their pains.

In this climate, it is not surprising that professionalism appeared in the Olympics within a few centuries after the first recorded games were held in 776 BC. Greek states bought and sold athletes, and the athletes changed allegiances to accommodate the highest bidder.

Celebrity-athletes were paid high fees to compete at local events. One record payment came to nearly 300 pounds of silver. In Athens a champion sprinter was awarded 1,200 drachmas for a race, enough to buy a luxurious home or a flock of 100 sheep and a half-dozen slaves to tend them. In time, professionalism became so commonplace that athletes in both Greece and Rome set up trade unions.

Although some historians argue that only a handful of cheating incidents occurred during the ancient games, the Greeks themselves said otherwise. Most cheating was punished by stiff fines, which were paid by sponsoring states and used to erect bronze statues of the gods. Athens, for example, paid for six such statues when its Olympic athlete Kallipos was caught bribing his opponents to let him win the pentathlon in the second half of the fourth century BC.

The most celebrated incident involved the Roman emperor Nero, who traveled to Greece to compete in the Olympic chariot races in AD 67. His was a difficult race. First, he fell out of his chariot. Helped back in, he still was unable to finish. Nevertheless the emperor was declared victorious—with the help of a 250,000-drachma bribe that induced the judges to proclaim that Nero deserved the wreath because he would have won if he had been able to finish. After Nero's death, however, the decision was ruled invalid and his name stricken from the record of victors. Simple chicanery was probably more the rule. For example, all Olympic athletes covered their bodies with olive oil, but wrestlers were required to dust themselves with powder so that their opponents could get a firm grip. But some of them, according to the playwright Aristophanes, would secretly wipe an oily hand over the areas of their bodies most likely to be clutched by an opponent.

The ancient games occasioned their share of political intrigue and at least once were a cause of war. In 420 BC, during the Peloponnesian War between Athens and Sparta, the Eleans—who controlled Olympia—sided with Athens and barred the Spartans from the Olympics. One Spartan charioteer, named Lichas, competed anyway, claiming to be from neutral Thebes. He won but was discovered and publicly whipped. The Spartans responded by attacking the Eleans.

In the end, the Olympics themselves fell victim to politics and changing times. In AD 393, not long before the old Roman Empire—heir to the lost grandeur of Greece—collapsed in the face of marauding hordes from the north, Rome's first Christian emperor, Theodosius I, abolished the games as a pagan holdover. By the time the Olympics were revived 1,500 years later, Olympia's temples, magnificent statuary, and elaborate sports facilities were no more. □

An Olympic Superstar

Milo of Crotona, who lived in the sixth century BC, may well have been the the world's first sports celebrity. He was certainly among the most enduring through legends of his athletic prowess and enormous strength.

Milo's fame was built around his domination of wrestling, in which he won five Olympic crowns and twenty-five victories in other championship contests before he retired. The story is told that he began training for each Olympic competition by carrying a newborn calf on his shoulders every day until the animal was fully grown.

This champion of wrestlers demonstrated his strength before 40,000 spectators at one Olympic festival by carrying a four-year-old heifer around the stadium, then killing it with one blow of his fist. After it had been cleaned and cooked, he ate the entire animal in a single day. Milo's regular daily diet included twenty pounds of wheat, another twenty of bread, and eighteen pints of wine.

Like numerous sports celebrities in later times, Milo married into a prominent family. His bride was the daughter of Pythagoras, the philosopher and mathematician, who also lived in Crotona. The father-in-law chose well, it is said, for the muscular Milo once saved the philosopher's life by supporting the entire roof of Pythagoras's house when it threatened to collapse. After owner and guests had safely fled, Milo relaxed his muscles, then strode unharmed from the falling debris.

This giant's death fostered a legend just as grand as his life. One day, the story goes, Milo was walking in the hills outside Crotona when he came upon a huge tree that had been cut down and partially split by a woodsman. The woodsman's wedges were still jammed in the trunk, prompting Milo to think that he could finish the job himself by thrusting his fingers into the split and prying outward. But nature conspired to defeat this master of the arena. As the split widened, the wedges fell out and the log snapped together, trapping Milo's fingers. By the time he was found, the great wrestler had been killed and partially eaten by wolves. □

Bare Facts

Greek men felt no shame at displaying their naked bodies, and all contestants in the Olympic Games competed in the nude. Indeed, the Greeks always looked on their readiness to strip in public as one of the traits that set them apart from uncouth barbarians.

No certain explanation has been offered for the code of athletic undress, but a cautionary tale by the poet Homer may account for it. In this story of competition, the contestants wore shorts—until one champion lost a race when he tripped over his dropping drawers.

A more plausible explanation might have been the great pride Greek men took in their bodies. Following the example of the Spartans, who dominated the Olympics, the athletes covered their bodies with olive oil, which kept dirt from getting into the pores and highlighted muscles. They also believed that the oil—carried in a special flask and wiped away after a contest with a curved metal scraper called a strigil (below)—made their skin more supple. □

Olympic Revels

The ancient Olympic Games were a grand festival, with myriad distractions for spectators and athletes. Vendors hawked food and other commodities, ranging from religious statues to horses. Acrobats, jugglers, sword swallowers, and conjurers entertained between events. And, since all Greeks loved a good tale, poets and writers declaimed their works from the porticoes of the Temple of Zeus. □

Aztec Gambling Fever

The Aztecs were among the most ardent high-stakes gamblers the world has ever known. Their favorite vehicle was a board game called Patolli, in which players cast dicelike marked beans to determine the progress of six colored markers over a cross-shaped playing surface (above, right).

A game of Patolli was a raucous occasion of joking, shouting, drinking, and desperate wagering. Indeed, it was not uncommon for players and spectators to bet all they owned—clothing, jewelry, home, lands, mistresses, children, and even their own freedom.

Such frantic gaming was spurred by far more than lust for winnings. In fact, it was an expression of religious belief, and heavy betting was almost mandatory in Aztec society; a reluctance to risk all was considered a lack of faith in the gods. Gambling was one way a man could learn how the gods felt about him—a consistent winner

was evidently favored, but a loser was not. At every cast of the marked beans, players invoked the gods—most often Macuilxochitl, the god of games and feasting (above, left), and Ometochtli, god of pulque, the fermented drink that was consumed in great quantities during Patolli play.

Patolli was so bound up with Aztec religion and culture that, for many players, it became a symbol of their own lives. For example, the Aztec calendar was based on a fifty-two-year cycle; there were fifty-two squares to be traversed during a game, and a victorious player could thus believe that the next fifty-two-year cycle would be a lucky one. But if victory assured the continuation of a happy life or the improvement of an unhappy one, defeat represented an end to joy or the continuation of de-

spair—and if a player lost his freedom, it could well mean death in a society that sometimes offered up slaves as sacrifices to the gods.

Disturbed by the religious implications of Patolli, early Christian missionaries did all they could to stamp it out. But the Aztecs continued to play in secret. Their descendants still play it today, but only as a harmless board game. □

In 2300 BC, the game Wei-qi was played in China's provinces to decide major issues such as the choice of rulers. This, the oldest known board game, is still popular today—known to its many fans as the game of go.

Bloody Spectacles

The most famous of all Roman games—fights to the death between combatants known as gladiators—began as a variation of an Etruscan funeral custom. In this ancient rite, men were sacrificed in mock combat so that the honored dead would have an armed escort for the journey into the next world.

The first gladiatorial contests in Rome were held at the city's cattle market in 264 BC to mark the funerals of certain aristocrats. There, slaves were forced to fight each other, apparently to honor the dead and divert the mourners. Because of the large crowds that were drawn to these battles, the contests were soon shifted to the far more spacious Roman Forum. Thus began a 600-year reign of wanton butchery staged to entertain an enthusiastic populace.

Gladiators were most often slaves and prisoners. They protected themselves with armor and shields and fought with weapons ranging from swords and javelins to three-pronged spears called tridents. Fearlessness and a lust for combat were demanded; anything less was rewarded with a whipping or prodding with a hot iron—means of forcing a reluctant gladiator into the arena.

At first, private citizens sponsored the contests; eventually, the state took over the games, which became ever more extravagant. Julius Caesar, for example, used the gigantic Circus Maximus in Rome to stage a full-scale battle, each army complete with 500 infantrymen, 60 cavalrymen, and 20 elephants. In order to accommodate the ever-grander contests, work began in the first century AD on the mammoth Colosseum, an architectural marvel that still stands in the heart of Rome.

To satisfy the public's increasing thirst for novelty, women and dwarfs were featured in gladiatorial combat. Forests were uprooted and replanted in the Colosseum to provide a properly primeval setting for contests between men and imported lions and tigers. Wild animals were unleashed to put criminals to death—in executions so horrible and humiliating that condemned prisoners sometimes took their own lives in order to avoid entering the arena.

Bloodlust was not all that brought Romans to such spectacles. There were also lotteries, with prizes ranging from elephants and ships to houses. And the armor of fallen gladiators was customarily tossed to the mob in the Colosseum's lower tiers, an act that frequently touched off frenzied battles over the spoils.

In time, the games went far beyond mere casual entertainment and became a principal part of the Romans' lives. By the middle of the first century AD, no fewer than ninety-three days were set aside each year as game days, when Roman citizens put in short workdays, then spent the remainder of their day at the arena. By the fourth century, the number of such days had nearly doubled.

Historians have been unable to agree on an explanation for Rome's infatuation with organized slaughter. Some speculate that the games had religious implications; others that they helped celebrate military victories or unify the people. As for the Romans themselves, they held that watching such grisly spectacles elevated the spirit. □

Rare Roman Pity

Seldom in the bloody history of the Roman games were spectators moved by compassion for the thousands of human beings and beasts who died for their entertainment. On one notable occasion, however, the mob took pity on its suffering victims—a dying herd of North African elephants.

The year was 79 BC, and the animals had been pitted against a band of the Getuli, a nomadic African people who carried javelins and shields on their hunts. It was a gory, one-sided contest, although one elephant, driven to its knees and with spears dangling from its huge body, did manage to pursue its tormentors, snatching away the tribesmen's shields and tossing them into the air. The crowd, thinking this was a planned trick, cheered. But not for long. As dying elephants trumpeted their agony, the spectators' mood changed to anger, and they demanded that the remaining animals be spared.

To be sure, the slaughter of animals was the rule rather than the exception. In some contests, unarmed men stunned bears with a blow of the fist or choked lions by jamming an arm into the animal's throat and grasping its tongue with the other hand. In others, the animals were pitted against one another. During the celebration of the opening of Rome's Colosseum in AD 81, nine thousand animals died—five thousand in one day. □

In this detail from a third-century-AD mosaic, hunters drive a procession of captured African beasts up a gangway for shipment to the arenas of Rome, where the animals would be slaughtered for the amusement of spectators.

An Imperial Bird Hunt

Some Roman emperors were content merely to sponsor games. Others—among them Commodus, who reigned in the late second century AD—chose to participate in the events. But Commodus's achievements were considerably less than heroic: On his most notable day, he stood with bow and arrows in his royal box at the Colosseum and slaughtered a hundred hapless ostriches. □

Early Soccer

During China's Han dynasty (207 BC to AD 220) two games were played that strongly resembled today's soccer. In one, players juggled, dribbled, and passed the ball from one to another without holding it in their hands. In the other game, they took turns kicking the ball at a target. □

Manhunting

The Etruscans—who flourished in western Italy during the seventh and sixth centuries BC—anticipated the gore of the Roman games with their own brutal sport of manhunting, seen above in an Etruscan tomb painting. At the end of this hunt, the leashed hound mauls a slave, who has a club but is blinded by a hood. The bearded hunter closes in to administer the *coup de grâce*, perhaps by strangling his quarry with the dog's leash. Such pastimes may have had roots in rituals of human sacrifice. □

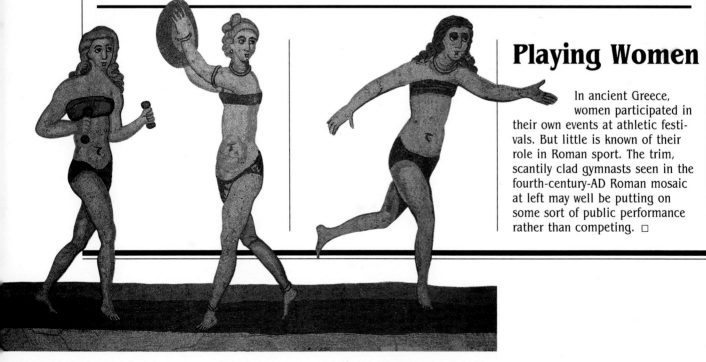

Playing Women

In ancient Greece, women participated in their own events at athletic festivals. But little is known of their role in Roman sport. The trim, scantily clad gymnasts seen in the fourth-century-AD Roman mosaic at left may well be putting on some sort of public performance rather than competing. □

At Sea in Rome

In their constant quest for novelty and spectacle in the games, the emperors of Rome ordered re-enactments of famous battles—including sea fights that were staged with full-size warships. Indeed, until the second century AD, when animal stalls were built beneath its arena floor, the Colosseum itself was sometimes the scene of these mock naval engagements.

Filling and draining the arena was a difficult task, however, and the scope of these watery combats was limited by the size of the Colosseum. So the emperors dug huge basins to accommodate the largest warships and allow ample room for maneuvers. Augustus, for example, ordered construction of a fifty-acre battle pond served by a specially built aqueduct that was nearly twelve miles in length. After one reenactment, in which as many as 3,000 gladiators fought in and over the water, the contents of the pond were used to provide water for the city.

No expense was spared to re-create a battle scene. Once, a fort was built on an island in the center of a basin so that an "Athenian" naval force could prevail over defending "Syracusans." Other re-creations called for bridges on which gladiators could fight to the death for the amusement of spectators lining the shore. □

Clad in the simple clothing of a noble captive, an eighth-century figurine of a Mayan ballplayer stands ready to begin a deadly game. The raised beads on the player's face mark ritual bloodletting.

A Deadly Ball Game

In the early sixteenth century, Hernán Cortés took his band of Spanish adventurers to the Aztec capital of Tenochitlan, site of today's Mexico City, in search of mountains of gold. What he found were heaps of human skulls displayed near the walled court in which was played a dangerous game of ball indeed: The losers often lost their heads. Variations of this grisly game, laden with religious symbolism, were played throughout pre-Columbian Mesoamerica, and some historians trace its origins back to the early Olmec Indians in about 2000 BC. It is thought that the contest symbolized the never-ending war between the forces of light and darkness, a kind of athletic morality play—in which, however, the forces of evil could occasionally triumph over those of good.

Details are sketchy, but it appears that in one version, as played by the Maya in southern Mexico, the game took place on a large flight of stairs. It is thought that the losers were bound tightly into a ball, then rolled down the stairs to death at the hands of a headsman.

More commonly, the game was played in a walled court. Opposing teams of up to seven players each sought to score points by shooting the grapefruit-size hard rubber ball through stone rings that were set high on the wall. Only the players' hips, feet, and elbows could contact the ball, which was not supposed to touch the ground.

The goal rings were so small and high that getting the ball ◊

through them was nearly impossible; the team that managed to do so was declared the winner immediately. Points were normally accumulated by hitting the rings or maneuvering the ball into other specified areas of the court. Sometimes the games were rigged by forcing captives—deliberately weakened by poor diet and perhaps torture—to play on the foreordained losing team.

If the ball game could be fatal to losers, it had its dangers for the victors too: A hard-hit ball could kill a player if it struck him solidly in the head or stomach. To protect themselves, the players wore heavy padding, most notably a horseshoe-shaped yoke of wood, wicker, or reeds wrapped around the waist. The midsection was protected by a flat stone fitted into the yoke, and the uniforms were completed by stone knee guards *(above)* and belts from which were hung effigies of opponents' heads.

Elaborately carved stone replicas of the yokes were worn in postgame ceremonies and were sometimes interred with the remains of sacrificial victims.

The games were often occasions for the frenzied gambling that seemed to be a passion among the Aztecs *(page 101)*. Once, two Aztec rulers bet their respective domains on the outcome of a single ball game. But the loser, rather than paying up, decided to have the winner assassinated.

Although Spanish missionaries did their best to eradicate the old Mesoamerican ball game, some remnants persist to this day in isolated Mexican villages. The modern version is called *ulama,* a less complicated approximation of the Aztec name, *ullamaliztli.* Today's game is less complicated in one other respect as well: The losing players live to play again. □

Pioneer Cardplayers

The Chinese were the first people to develop playing cards, sometime before the ninth century AD. As entertainment, they considered the games that were played with these slender slips of cardboard superior to many other diversions.

In the somewhat enigmatic words of one early enthusiast, cards could be "played by a group of four without annoying conversation, and without the difficulties which accompanied playing chess or meditation." □

VOYAGERS

The course of cultural evolution down through history and across the world has long fascinated scholars, who tend to explain advances in two distinct ways. One holds that societies have matured independently, evolving from nomadic tribes into settled communities—and sometimes great civilizations—in relative isolation. Cultures geographically close no doubt exchanged certain traits, this theory goes, but not until the great voyages of discovery in the fifteenth and sixteenth centuries was there cross-cultural exchange on a global scale. Before then, if widely separated peoples happened to grow along similar lines, it was a coincidence, most scholars think—and not a surprising one. The human mind, after all, does not vary biologically, regardless of divergent surroundings. Faced with similar challenges, therefore, a native of the Arctic tundra might well come up with much the same solutions as a native of the American desert or the Asian steppes.

The second view of cultural development is more speculative and relies on bits of evidence scattered throughout the world—customs shared by tribal peoples separated by thousands of miles, plants growing far from their native soil, artifacts bearing inscriptions alien to the lands where they are found. Such clues suggest that cultural characteristics have been transmitted by transoceanic visitations all but lost in the mists of history.

It is known today, of course, that Norsemen preceded Columbus to America. But there are those who suggest that, hundreds of years before the Norse, Buddhist monks from Asia visited a new world they called Fu Sang and left their mark on its native cultures. They were followed soon after, some say, by an Irish saint named Brendan who crossed the Atlantic in an ox-hide boat, as the illumination from a medieval German manuscript *(above)* depicts.

Those who believe in such early travels challenge the view that cross-cultural pollination began with the great Renaissance voyages of Columbus, Balboa, and Magellan. Rather, these theorists say, societies in many parts of the world matured by learning from each other—a process spawned by numerous, if unrecorded, voyages of the distant past.

A Norse Incursion?

On a 200-pound chunk of gray sandstone supposedly unearthed from Minnesota farmland, a strange tale is inscribed. In 1362, the story goes, a band of Scandinavians—eight Swedes and twenty-two Norwegians—sailed the Atlantic to explore North America. They landed safely and then pushed their way westward into what is now Minnesota, where tragedy struck. One day when twenty of the explorers were off fishing, the ten who stayed behind were massacred by Indians. When the fishing party returned, it found the slaughtered comrades and fled in terror.

The yarn is chilling, but is it history or hoax? Either way, it first came to light one November morning in 1898 when a Swedish immigrant named Olof Ohman and his ten-year-old son Edward were clearing a grove of trees on their farm near Kensington, Minnesota. While uprooting an aspen, the pair saw tangled in the tree's roots a stone some thirty inches long, sixteen inches wide, and five and one-half inches thick. The bottom and one side were covered with a curious inscription.

When news of the discovery reached the public, its reception was about as friendly as that supposedly accorded the Norse explorers by the local Indians. Scholars called in to inspect the Kensington stone, as it came to be known, scoffed at the idea that it might be a genuine fourteenth-century relic inscribed by visiting Norsemen in the ancient runic writing of their people. Had it been authentic, it might have made the case that Scandinavians not only preceded Christopher Columbus to America by a good many years but managed to explore hundreds of miles inland. But the investigators—including academicians from both American and Scandinavian universities—pronounced the stone a crude hoax. Linguists scoffed, noting that the inscription had many grammatical inconsistencies.

Olof Ohman quickly came under fire from skeptics who asserted that he had carved the stone himself. Upset over the accusations, the quiet Swede retrieved his stone and unceremoniously used it as a doorstep for his granary. There it stood in 1907, when a Norwegian-born writer and lecturer by the name of Hjalmar Rued Holand paid Ohman a visit. Defying the academicians, Holand championed the Kensington stone's authenticity. For more than half a century, until his death in 1963, he tirelessly tried to convince the world that the stone was genuine.

Despite his many critics, Holand did manage to have the Smithsonian Institution exhibit the stone in 1948 and 1949. One of the museum's directors called it "probably the most important archaeological object yet found in North America." But his opinion was by no means universal. Among other arguments, critics noted that the stone's inscription was remarkably unweathered for its purported great age.

Still, the favorable notice was enough to resurrect interest in the stone, and opinions pro and con have led to a plethora of books and articles about it by scientists and laypeople. In a 1982 book, *The Kensington Rune-Stone Is Genuine*, for example, Robert Hall, a professor emeritus of linguistics at Cornell University, asserts the stone's authenticity. Another defender, amateur Danish linguist Richard Neilsen, has published a series of painstakingly documented articles in scholarly journals, claiming that new linguistic evidence proves all the runes on the Kensington stone are authentic fourteenth-century forms.

While the controversy continues, the Kensington stone lies in a modest museum in Alexandria, Minnesota. Watched over by the local Chamber of Commerce, it silently guards its secret. □

Goodbye Columbus

Called by some individuals "the most exciting cartographic discovery of the century" and by others an ingenious forgery, a crude parchment map may hold the key to the question of who really discovered America.

The worn document, known as the Vinland map, is thought by some experts to have been painted by a Swiss monk around 1440. Its name comes from a Latin inscription in its top left corner claiming that the legendary Viking Leif Eriksson "discovered a new land, extremely fertile and even having vines, the which island they named Vinland." Roughly but surely, the map of the world shows this island— labeled Vinilanda Insula—to be North America. If the map is genuine, it is the only known one to

pinpoint the location of America prior to Columbus's 1492 voyage.

In 1957, rare-book dealer Laurence Witten of New Haven, Connecticut, bought the map from a European dealer for $3,500. It came bound with a manuscript called *The Tartar Relation*, a thirteenth-century narrative of a Central Asian journey. Witten later received a fragment of a medieval encyclopedia that seemed to ◊

have been written by the same person who penned *The Tartar Relation*. When he placed the three documents on top of one another, he was amazed to find that wormholes in all three matched, indicating they came from a single bound document. If the map had been compiled with works some two centuries older, Witten reasoned, it must also be very old—and almost surely genuine.

Witten's find went largely unnoticed until 1965, when Yale University put its considerable academic prestige behind the map's authenticity. An anonymous buyer had purchased the chart and its two related documents from Witten and donated them to the school, whose scholars subsequently declared that the Vinland map had indeed been drawn in the fifteenth century. They wrote a book called *The Vinland Map and Tartar Relation,* which concluded that the map was "the oldest surviving map of American lands."

The book made headlines around the world. While several Norse sagas tell of a land called Vinland—and many experts were already convinced that the Vikings had preceded Columbus there by many years—the parchment map was apparently the earliest graphic evidence of such a place. "Somehow a map cannot lie," one expert wrote; "an account can. To the man in the street the description of Vinland in the sagas is so many words; the description of Vinland by a line drawing is a revelation."

But was it? After the Yale findings, a team of independent investigators examined the map and found that its ink contained traces of anatase, a form of titanium dioxide that had not been developed before the 1920s. Thus, adjudged this research team, the Vinland map was a forgery.

But the controversy surrounding the map was not over. In 1985, scientists from respected Crocker Nuclear Laboratory at the University of California at Davis subjected the map to two days of stringent testing, including 159 particle-induced x-ray emission analyses. From its study, this group concluded that the 1974 tests were faulty and that "the prior interpretation that the map has been shown to be a twentieth-century forgery must be reevaluated."

Neither vindicated nor debunked, the Vinland map still lies at Yale, hinting—but not yet offering absolute graphic proof—that the Norse were pre-Columbian voyagers to the New World. □

Looks Are Not Everything

The strong features of the six-inch marble head shown at left look distinctly African. But the head, dating from about AD 600, is the work of a Mexican artist.

Many such pre-Columbian artworks have either an African or an Oriental cast, and some researchers see this fact as evidence that Africans and Asians long ago traveled to the shores of the Gulf of Mexico and influenced the native cultures there. In the absence of other compelling evidence, however, most archaeologists consider such conclusions to be unwarranted. The people of any given culture, they point out, can have a wide variety of physical characteristics, some of which might seem at first glance to be peculiar to a different, distant race. And in any case, artists throughout the ages have frequently been guided by personal vision and individual whim, and they have not necessarily painted or sculpted exactly what they have seen. □

The Riddle of the Well-Traveled Maize

The familiar maize plant—better known to Americans as corn—has generated a spirited scholarly debate that centers on the possibility of ancient, unrecorded sea travel. Botanists know that maize cannot propagate itself; its occurrence must therefore be the result of human agency. They also know that the plant originated in the New World. And yet, some researchers have found evidence that it appeared elsewhere well before the known voyages of discovery linked Old World and New.

That anomalous evidence includes reports that maize preceded the arrival of Europeans in East Africa in the late fifteenth century. Just how it got there, the natives could not say at the time, for they had cultivated it for many generations. Similarly, West Africans could only point north and east when asked about the origin of their maize—and the trail in that direction dwindled in the sands of the Sahara.

Even more intriguing is evidence that maize was well established in Asia long before Columbus's voyages. Eleventh-century temples in southern India, where maize was supposedly unknown at the time, house many stone figures that, according to some cultural geographers, are offering ears of maize to the gods *(right)*. Other experts dispute this interpretation of the Indian art, claiming that the objects are pomegranates or beaded ornaments. Perhaps the debate will someday be resolved, but for now the path that maize followed across the world remains a blurred and dim one. □

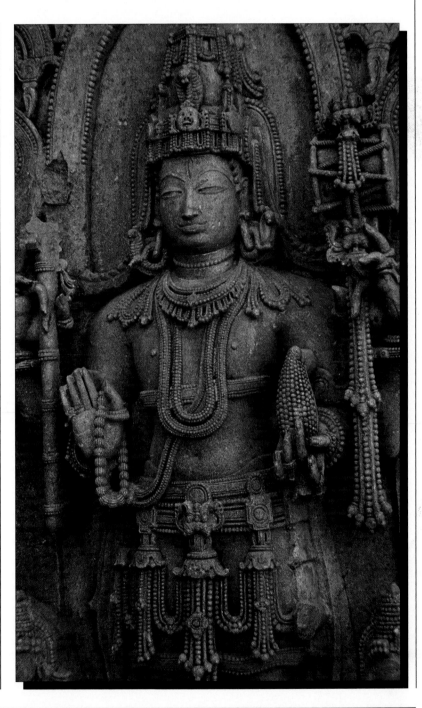

Meaningful Gestures

Although found half a world apart, a sixth-century Chinese Buddha *(below, left)* and an eighth-century Mayan maize god *(below, right)* exhibit mirror-image gestures.

Used ritually, such hand gestures are called mudras in the Orient. Throughout the Buddhist and Hindu worlds, there are dozens of gestures and body positions with symbolic meaning, and the ancient mudras persist today. Friends often greet each other with a praying-hands gesture, a mudra of reverence and respect.

The mudras of religious icons signal their benefit to worshipers. This Buddha's outstretched left hand says he is bestowing a gift; his upraised right hand signifies the gift is courage. Although the hand positions of the Mayan statue are reversed, the similarity is thought by some scholars to be too great to be coincidence. Indeed, the hand postures are among several similarities between Asian and New World icons that some researchers see as evidence that pre-Columbian cultures of the Americas may have been influenced by Asian visitors. Parallels have been found in costumes, headdresses, ornaments, physiques, and body positions of religious statues on both sides of the Pacific. □

The Ancient Hebrews of Tennessee

Throughout the river valleys of the southeastern United States lie hundreds of man-made earthen mounds in which American Indians laid their dead to rest. But in one such mound, according to some researchers, there are non-Indian remains as well—the bones of Jewish refugees who may have fled the brutal Roman occupation of Palestine in the first century AD.

This tomb first came to light in 1889, when a team from the Smithsonian Institution excavated three burial mounds along Bat Creek in Loudon County, Tennessee. Nine skeletons were found in one mound, two of them set apart from the other seven. Beneath one of these two skeletons lay several unusual artifacts, among them a stone tablet bearing nine carved letters.

The director of the mound excavation project, a man by the name of Cyrus Thomas, decided that the inscription contained letters of the Cherokee alphabet, which had been devised around 1820 by the Cherokee scholar Sequoya. The bones and the tablet were sent to the Smithsonian for later consideration; Thomas published his report in 1894, and there the matter seemed to rest.

But in the 1950s, archaeologist Joseph Mahan happened upon a picture of the Bat Creek tablet and reached a conclusion remarkably more exotic than Thomas's. Mahan knew the Cherokee alphabet and, as he wrote later, could see "no relationship whatever between the symbols on the stone and those developed by Sequoya." What Mahan did see, upon turning the picture of the stone upside down, was a striking similarity between several of the letters and ancient Canaanite writing.

No expert in Semitic languages, Mahan sent a photograph to Semitic language scholar Cyrus Gordon, who confirmed Mahan's observation. The characters, said Gordon, were from a Hebrew dialect dating to about the first century AD. They translated as "A Comet for the Jews." He speculated that one of the skeletons was that of a leader—the "comet" memorialized by the tablet.

Others who have compared the inscription with Cherokee, Paleo-Hebrew, and English characters take the position that, on the basis of their shapes, the carvings are as similar to English letters as to Cherokee characters—but are even more like Hebrew, as Gordon said. Support for Gordon's assessment also comes from carbon-14 dating of wood fibers found with the skeletons. These tests reveal that the bodies were buried sometime in the first two centuries AD.

To be sure, there are many reasons to question the scenario suggested by Gordon's translation of the inscription. For example, the other artifacts recovered at the Bat Creek grave site are clearly American Indian rather than Hebraic. And there is, of course, no hint in voluminous Hebrew lore of how any ancient Hebrews might have come to be among the Indians of Tennessee 1,900 years ago. □

Modern seafaring indicates that ancient peoples could have crossed oceans despite the smallness of their boats. In recent years, the Atlantic has been traversed by, among other things, two rafts, two dugout canoes, two dories propelled only by oars, several dories with sails, and a conventional sailboat less than six feet long.

The Fabled Voyage of Brendan

A monument to the storytelling art of the Irish people, the chronicle of Saint Brendan tells of an abbot and seventeen monks who journeyed to the "promised land of the saints" during a seven-year sojourn in a leather boat. "The Voyage of the Holy Abbot Brendan" was written in Latin during the ninth or tenth century, some 300 to 400 years after the death of Brendan. Most scholars consider the story merely an outstanding example of religious allegory. Some historians, however, suggest that the allegory contains seeds of truth—evidence that Brendan was in the vanguard of Irish sailors who explored the New World long before other Europeans.

It is arguable that the abbot and his contemporaries had boats equal to the trip. The crafts were constructed of hides stretched over wooden frames and waterproofed with animal fat. They must have been quite durable, since Irish sailors of Brendan's day are known to have traveled the rough waters surrounding the British Isles, venturing at least as far as Iceland. There is speculation that Brendan himself might have been one of these doughty voyagers.

That the boats were capable of sailing across the Atlantic was demonstrated in 1977 by British sailor Timothy Severin, who made the 2,600-mile journey from Ireland to Newfoundland in a thirty-six-foot ox-hide craft (right). Dubbed the Brendan, the boat was built to medieval specifications.

Brendan's own voyage, described in the fanciful Latin account, was a nonstop adventure. Each Easter for at least five years, the holy man and his crew supposedly conducted their celebrations while aground on the back of a whale. They visited an island packed with snow-white sheep, and on another island, throngs of birds chanted prayers with them. The monks spent twenty days becalmed on a "coagulated sea" and sailed eight days on waters so clear that they could see to the sandy bottom, where fish lay curled like cats, heads touching their tails.

The crew encountered wild beasts, a pillar of crystal, and an island of fire. Almost always in imminent danger, it seemed, they were invariably rescued from disaster by Brendan's prayers. Eventually, the company made it to the promised land, where they spent forty days and nights gathering wonderful fruits and precious stones before returning home.

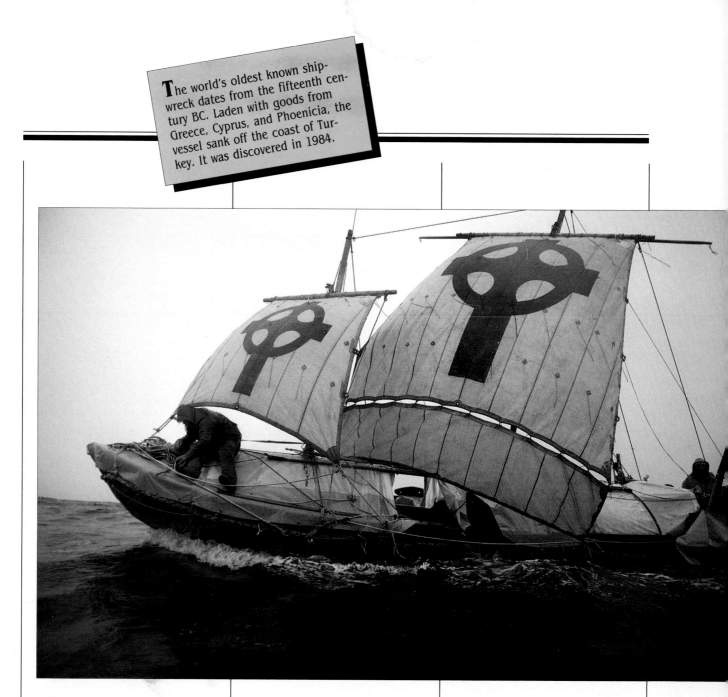

Modern researchers find in Brendan's story tantalizing hints that the saint indeed visited exotic lands. The clear sea, they say, could have been the sparkling waters of the Bahamas. The fiery island could describe volcanic Iceland—where Irish monks are known to have settled. The pillar of crystal may have been an iceberg, and the coagulated sea could have been the algae-choked Sargasso,

so dreaded by later seafarers.

These speculations find support in certain documents and traditions dating from shortly before the time of Columbus. Maps of the day often placed Brendan's promised land at a spot slightly west of the Canary Islands. The Spanish and Portuguese both sent expeditions to find Brendan's Isle as late as the sixteenth century.

The Renaissance mariners' con-

clusion—seconded by some modern authors—is that the monks' expedition reached the shores of the St. Johns River at St. Augustine, Florida, where the Spaniard Juan Ponce de León would later search for the fountain of youth. Nevertheless, skeptics maintain that Saint Brendan's voyage was simply a well-told tale, no less a fable than Ponce de León's forever elusive fountain. □

A Mystery of Monks and Megaliths

Scattered on a rocky rise of ground near North Salem, New Hampshire, is one of the more intriguing of America's archaeological oddities—a grouping of cavelike structures that have suggested to some people that venturesome Europeans settled in the New World long before Columbus.

Appropriately known later as Mystery Hill, the place had no name when a farmer, Jonathan Pattee, moved there in 1826. It was still nameless when Pattee died in 1848, but the rumors were starting. Locals speculated about what use Pattee might have made of the apparent caves on the hill. Some said he sheltered runaway slaves there; others guessed that the caves were where the farmer hid his moonshine whiskey. Both stories missed the real puzzle of the hill: questions not about what the so-called caves sheltered but about what they actually were and who had built them.

In fact, they were not caves at all but arrangements of huge rocks. They looked like megalithic ruins—twenty-two structures sprawling across one acre, with outlying stones covering another twelve acres. In the central area, boulders weighing at least five tons lay atop vertical stone slabs, and smaller stones made up arched rooms that were covered over with earth. Amid scattered rocks lay a tablelike slab *(above)* that looked, some said, like a sacrificial altar.

In Britain and elsewhere in Europe, megalithic monuments are not uncommon, but only a few such structures have been found in the New World. Small wonder, then, that the stones on Pattee's old homestead continued to arouse curiosity over the years, finally igniting a near-frenzy of enthusiasm in an amateur archaeologist by the name of William B. Goodwin when he visited the site in 1933. A wealthy retired insurance executive from Hartford, Connecticut, Goodwin took one look and announced that Pattee's caves were, in fact, the remains of a tenth-century monastery established by Irish monks who had fled the Viking invasions of their homeland. This conclusion caused something of a stir in academic circles, as well as in the press.

Goodwin soon bought the place and began cleaning it up and "restoring" it to what he felt must have been its original condition. Much debris was discarded—possibly including artifacts that might have helped determine with certainty the stones' true origins. Massive stones were lifted atop others and rooms were rebuilt. So clumsy and extensive was the work that Goodwin, who had brought the site to the world's attention, also effectively obliterated any chance of finding out the truth about its origins.

Thus a mystery it remained, officially becoming Mystery Hill in name as well as fact in 1957 when Robert E. Stone, another antiquarian, bought the property after Goodwin's death.

Later digs, far more careful than Goodwin's, have yielded no ancient artifacts, and attempts to date the site have been inconclusive. Carbon-14 dating, which cannot be used on stone, was applied to pieces of charcoal found in the area. One bit of charcoal, found beneath a stone wall, was found to date from 1500 BC. However, the piece could just as easily have been the by-product of an ancient forest fire as the leavings of a prehistoric campfire. Eight similar tests were made. Two yielded prehistoric dates, but the other six were from much more recent history—the eighteenth and nineteenth centuries.

Barry Fell, a retired professor of biology at Harvard University, has devoted considerable time to the riddle of Mystery Hill, focusing most of his energies on obscure carvings and inscriptions that he discerns on some of the stones. Fell theorizes that the markings represent an ancient Celtic language called Ogam, indicating to Fell that Mystery Hill's beginnings may date anywhere from 800 BC to the third century AD, considerably earlier than Goodwin's tenth-century Irish monks.

Most archaeologists, though, refuse to accept such findings. They conclude more prosaically that the structures were built by New Hampshire farmers—perhaps in the colonial period or perhaps later by Pattee himself—in order to store roots and vegetables and to shelter cattle. □

Pytheas in Britain and Beyond

In his own time, the Greek navigator Pytheas was a target of scientific scorn. Today, he is revered as one of the ancient world's most acute observers.

By the beginning of the third century BC, this native of Marseilles had circumnavigated Britain, measured it, met its people, noted the farming and tin-mining techniques, and made astronomical observations that would aid navigators for centuries to come.

Pytheas correctly located the North Star, identified the relationship between the moon and the tides, and calculated the latitude of Marseilles.

Even so, for generations Pytheas's findings were roundly dismissed by other scholars. In fact, Greek and Roman sages of the next three centuries—Strabo, Polybius, and Pliny, among them—flatly declared him a liar.

Perhaps the problem was that Pytheas was too good a scientist, reporting everything he saw and heard, no matter how unusual. He saw ice floating in the sea; this sounded preposterous to Mediterranean people. He reported hearing about islands farther north than Britain, where summer nights lasted only two or three hours; that was deemed absurd.

Despite Pytheas's pathfinding voyage, nearly two centuries passed before the next Mediterranean sailors ventured north to Britain. But when they did, they relied on Pytheas's reports to lead them. □

Phoenicians in America?

"We are sons of Canaan from Sidon," begins the manuscript. It is written in a Phoenician language used some 500 years before the birth of Christ. In only eight lines, it tells a story of a voyage around Africa, of storm, human sacrifice, and salvation on the shores of what is now Brazil.

If it was indeed left by a Phoenician sailor, the text memorializes an ancient visit to the New World long suspected by some scholars. If not, the Paraíba Inscription, as it is called, is among history's more intriguing hoaxes.

In 1872, Ladislau Neto, the director of Brazil's National Museum of Rio de Janiero, received from a colleague a copy of a letter. Its author, who was never found, described a stone tablet unearthed by workers on a plantation in Paraíba—now called João Pessoa—at Brazil's easternmost tip. Neto, putting aside his initial doubts about the inscription, published the text in 1874, after unsuccessfully seeking the original tablet and the letter writer.

The inscription was promptly branded a fraud by experts in Phoenician languages, and a long-simmering public debate ensued. Finally Neto himself, after ten years of professional and personal agony, recanted his belief in the text's authenticity.

Until the late 1960s, the case seemed settled and was virtually forgotten. Then, Cyrus Gordon, an American scholar of Semitic languages, studied the text and declared it authentic—ironically, for some of the same reasons that it was adjudged fraudulent nearly a century before.

So-called inaccuracies of vocabulary and grammar cited by critics in 1874 had become, by 1968, mere idiosyncracies of dialect. Similarities between the inscription and ancient Hebrew, once considered evidence of deceit, had since been documented as normal among Phoenicians, a people who mixed readily with a number of other cultures.

Moreover, Gordon's analysis seemed to reveal no fewer than three cryptograms buried in the tale. One, typical of ancient scripts, includes numbers that, when added, confirm the date given by the writer. The other codes, according to Gordon, tell the story once again from the point of view of both a Canaanite pagan and a Jewish crewman. The cryptograms, he claimed, were evidence of authenticity, since few counterfeiters were likely to have taken such pains with their work.

To be sure, Gordon's detailed interpretation has not settled the controversy over the Paraíba Inscription, and the debate is likely to continue until—if ever—the original stone inscription can be found and judged. □

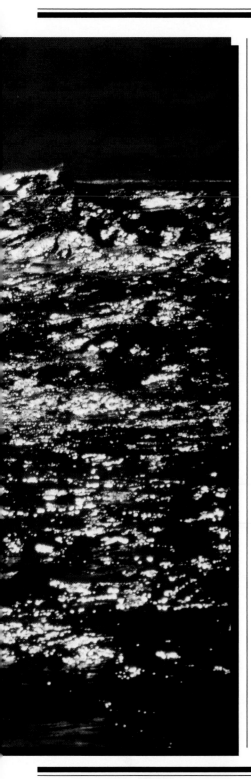

The Venturesome Polynesians

When Europeans began exploring the Polynesian Pacific in the eighteenth century, they found that they were not the first ones to call on the islands. Even on tiny, isolated coral atolls and volcanic rocks where no one lived to greet them, the sailors of England, Spain, and Portugal found the abandoned dwellings and temples of early colonists.

The Polynesian islands are scattered across a vast triangle whose corners are Hawaii, Easter Island, and New Zealand. Most are isolated from one another, sometimes separated by a thousand miles of ocean. Yet, by the time the first European visitors arrived, Polynesians had evidently been traveling among the islands for centuries.

Impressed, the Europeans praised the islanders' sailing skill and told tales of epic voyages. But later generations were skeptical. To achieve the feats attributed to them, it was pointed out, the Polynesians would have required supreme navigational skills—talents that seemed questionable, since the Polynesians knew nothing of charts, compasses, sextants, and the other staples of the sailor's art. Moreover, to travel eastward from what is now believed to have been their original home on the Asian mainland, they must somehow have known how to sail against trade winds and prevailing currents, which flow westward.

In 1968 and 1969, New Zealand yachtsman David Lewis set out to prove that the ancient islanders had indeed been supersailors. For nine months, Lewis and two Polynesian guides sailed back and forth across the Polynesian Pacific without compass or other instruments. Other, later voyages have also tended to establish the exceptional skills of the islanders.

Using seafaring lore passed down for countless generations, the native navigators are extraordinarily adept at using stars to fix their location and guide their way. They mark their position and progress by the rising and setting of certain stars, having memorized the positions of hundreds of them. Their charts are in their heads, and they recall the most minute details of islands, shoals, currents, and reefs. Their knowledge allows the Polynesians to navigate difficult channels and to land on islands that sit alone amid vast stretches of empty ocean.

They are also guided by the pattern of ocean swells that are shaped by islands many miles away, by the look of clouds, and by the flight of seabirds.

As for sailing against currents and trade winds, the island navigators rely on a sophisticated knowledge of ocean weather. Polynesians have apparently known for centuries that the weather systems that sweep across the Pacific cause the winds to reverse for as long as a week at a time. The reversal provides the patient sailor with a favorable wind.

Although the issue is far from settled, enough is known of the voyaging skills of the Polynesians to conclude that they could have ventured well beyond their island realm, sailing to the New World and back sometime in the unrecorded past. □

Against a threatening sky, a replica of an ancient Polynesian sailing canoe voyages through Pacific waters, navigated only by the pattern of ocean swells.

Roman Coins in America

Hundreds, perhaps thousands, of ancient Roman coins have turned up at various sites in the United States, among them a garden in Oshkosh, Wisconsin; a streambed near Black Mountain, North Carolina; and a field just outside Phenix City, Alabama.

Some researchers maintain that such finds are proof of European visits to the New World in antiquity. Skeptics counter that the coins have never been found with other artifacts that might support these claims. They also note that the reports seem to have proliferated after the two world wars—when veterans returning from Europe might have brought home souvenir coins that were later lost. □

Death-Dealing Clue to Pacific Voyages

The blowgun—accurate, silent, and deadly—is found in many parts of the world. But in tropical Asia and South America, the designs are so alike that some anthropologists propose that the weapon must have been carried to the New World by its Asian inventors, perhaps as many as 6,000 years ago.

The chief proponent of this theory is Stephen C. Jett, a geographer at the University of California at Davis. In a study lasting more than thirty years, Jett has examined hundreds of blowgun reports from explorers and anthropologists. And although some scholars remain skeptical of the geographer's conclusions, none has refuted his specific findings.

A rudimentary blowgun can be made by simply rolling a leaf to form a tube, but the weapon is usually considerably more complex. Jett discovered that blowguns in regular use by ancient peoples in Asia and South America were elaborate and multiform—and, in all their variations, remarkably similar from culture to culture.

The guns could be as short as eighteen inches, Jett found, or as long as twenty-three feet. The most complex ones were made of nested tubes, whose inner barrels were composed of one or two carefully fitted bamboo stems that provided a smooth passage for the projectile. The inner barrels were set inside outer barrels of rigid bamboo or of palm stem. Other guns were made of palm stems that were split, hollowed out, and then rejoined with glue and wrapped with bark.

In all, Jett was able to compare fifty-nine characteristics of the construction and use of blowguns, finding in the process that virtually all types of the weapon had been used on both sides of the Pacific, and used in similar ways for similar purposes.

Both Asian and American blowguns featured sights to help aim them, and the largest often had curved bores to compensate for the inevitable sag in their long barrels. Carved, painted, or inlaid decorations occasionally adorned blowguns of both hemispheres. And, wherever the weapons were found, mouthpieces of various kinds helped make them more efficient. In both Asia and America, a variety of projectiles were used, including darts dipped in poison derived from tree sap.

To Jett, the similarities are telling: Eighty-six percent of the traits of American blowguns are found in Asia. Either American technology developed along a remarkably parallel path or—more likely, says Jett—South American Indians learned much from Asian mentors who somehow made their way across the vast Pacific Ocean. □

The Rabbit in the Moon

From earliest times, people have gazed up at the moon and seen images in its shadowed landscape. In fact, no fewer than thirty creatures and artifacts are associated by various cultures with the patterns formed by the lunar mountains and valleys.

To modern Western eyes, few lunar images might seem less likely than the lowly rabbit. And yet, ancient cultures on opposite sides of the world saw that very animal—a fact that some believe helps prove long-ago contact between peoples of Asia and those of Mesoamerica.

In the years between the birth of Jesus of Nazareth and the arrival of the Spanish in the sixteenth century, the rabbit-in-the-moon motif was ubiquitous in the art of the Mixtec, Maya, Aztec, and other indigenous cultures of Central America. The same theme was common in China during the Han dynasty, which ruled from 207 BC to AD 220, and the Chinese apparently inherited the image from early cultures of India.

To be sure, a symbol's appearance in several cultures is not, in itself, persuasive evidence of trans-oceanic contact. But the sundry rabbits in the moon had several things in common in all the societies where the image appeared, and this intrigues anthropologists exploring the possibility of ancient voyages across the Pacific.

On both sides of the world, there are striking similarities in the myths surrounding the motif: In China, the rabbit was placed on the moon by Buddha as a reward for sacrificing itself so the Holy One could eat. The Aztec legend also involved a rabbit being sent skyward by a god, in this case a disgruntled deity who was trying to dim the light of a second sun. The rabbit accomplished the desired effect, in the process transforming the extra sun into the moon.

Moreover, in the tradition of both Old World and New, the rabbit is associated with intoxication and drugs. Banners and stone carvings in China show hares grinding the mushrooms used for ceremonial drugs. In India, the moon god, Soma, was a patron of liquor and drugs. Similarly, the Aztec moon goddess, Mayauel, held sway over revelry and drunkenness.

Some scholars believe that these correspondences must be more than coincidental. The rabbit in the moon, they contend, is part of a complex of evidence indicating that by the first century AD, Asian mariners had exported certain customs and beliefs to Mesoamerica. □

A number of ancient peoples may have had the ability to plot a course across the seas. Stars were used as navigational aids in a number of seafaring societies as early as the sixth century BC.

Ancient artists' renderings from China (above) and Mesoamerica (top) show the rabbit in the moon. To some researchers, the similar motifs suggest an early contact between the cultures.

A Paper Trail from Asia to the Americas

Wherever in the world humans have lived near tropical forests, it seems, they have sooner or later learned to use trees to make cloth and paper. The basic processes of stripping, softening, drying, and finishing the bark are simple enough, but they can have scores of intricate variations.

A few decades ago, the widespread but differing nature of this technology caught the imagination of the anthropologist Paul Tolstoy. He undertook to learn everything there is to know about how ancient tropics dwellers made cloth and paper. After studying the relics of cultures all over the world, he decided that, in all likelihood, long-ago seafarers from Southeast Asia brought the art of papermaking to the middle Americas.

In reaching this intriguing conclusion, Tolstoy charted the 119 possible features of bark paper manufacturing and correlated them with the practices of fifty-nine ancient societies. He tallied similarities and differences and found varying degrees of both. Finally, he pinpointed a papermaking connection between certain communities of central Mexico and villages of Celebes, now called Sulawesi, an Indonesian island east of Borneo.

Tolstoy's statistics were striking: Of the 119 manufacturing characteristics, 92 were shared by the cultures of central Mexico and Celebes. Moreover, two-thirds of the common characteristics had rarely occurred in the other areas of the world.

In both Celebes and central Mexico, for example, papermakers boiled their bark in an alkaline mixture of water and wood ashes. The boiling process itself is fairly rare among other bark-using peoples, and the use of identical mixtures in this manufacturing step seems beyond mere happenstance. For the subsequent beating, both cultures used grooved stone racquets with flexible handles. In addition, both of them joined pieces of bark by felting them, or beating their edges together so that fibers intertwined.

To the layperson, these similarities alone might seem to lie well outside the possibility of mere coincidence. But Tolstoy, a careful scientist, reasoned otherwise. Since types of beaters and methods of softening and joining were major influences on the finished product, the anthropologist conjectured, it was possible—however unlikely—that two widely separated societies might devise identical tools and strategies, given identical challenges.

So thinking, he sought to pinpoint trivial or arbitrary factors—equipment that could be used or procedures that could be done in almost any fashion, or eliminated entirely, without affecting the quality of the product or ease of processing. But even in this more stringent test, the commonalities held: The two societies seemed to have identical routines for the most arbitrary tasks. For example, both used a special board rather than a log or other surface on which to beat the bark.

Along with method, timing seems to support Tolstoy's argument that the art of bark processing made the journey

Although one is missing a handle, bark beaters from Celebes *(right)* and Mexico *(left)* exhibit similar design. Both are rectangular with grooves on top and bottom, and both took a handle. The implements were used in nearly identical bark papermaking processes on opposite sides of the globe.

from Southeast Asia to central Mexico. Surviving tools and samples of Asian bark cloth and paper date to between 2000 and 1000 BC. The first evidence of bark processing in Mexico is dated a thousand years later.

Paul Tolstoy's diligent scholarship and his stature as professor of anthropology at the University of Montreal have helped muster support for his theory from many of his colleagues in the field. Even so, although he himself is certain of his findings, Tolstoy makes no outsize claims for the theory built on his painstaking research. "I would not consider it proven," he comments. "In our field, I don't think there is too much that can be proven." □

Romans in Brazil

Relics of the days of colonial rule, the remains of more than 100 English, French, and Portuguese ships lie buried in the mud of Rio de Janiero's harbor. Among the wrecks, though, is one anomalous ruin that could challenge the accepted history of South American discovery. It is, some believe, the carcass of a Roman trading ship from the third century AD.

In 1976, a Brazilian diver working in Guanabara Bay, about fifteen miles from Rio, came to the surface with two large amphorae—tall stoneware jars used by ancient Mediterranean seafarers to store such things as water and oil. The government confiscated the jars, whereupon the diver refused to disclose where he had found them.

In 1982, however, he led an American underwater archaeologist, Robert Marx, to the find. Marx retrieved thousands of pottery fragments and more than 200 necks of amphorae from the silt. Working from photographs, Elizabeth Will, a professor of classical studies at the University of Massachusetts at Amherst and an expert on amphorae, dated the jars to the third century AD and pinpointed their origin to the old Roman city of Kouass on

the Moroccan coast.

Marx also probed the harbor floor with sonar and located the remains of a wooden ship—presumably the Roman trader—buried beneath a sixteenth-century wreck.

But before more conclusive exploration could be done, the Brazilian government ordered a halt. Local historians with sentimental ties to Brazil's mother country, Portugal, were outraged at the potential assault on their history. The Portuguese assert that the first European to land on Brazilian soil was Pedro Álvars Cabral. The story is disputed by the Spanish, who say their own Vicente Yáñez Pinzón was first. Both landed sometime in 1500.

In any event, Spain and Portugal became involved in the case, accusing Marx of being an agent of the Italian government—which was, supposedly, bent on establishing claim to an early Roman discovery of the New World. And Brazilian archaeologists, who had once identified the amphorae as Greek or Phoenician, began branding Robert Marx a sensation-seeking fortune hunter.

Other archaeologists are more

open-minded about the wreck's origin. They point to the fact that Roman wrecks have been found as far west as the Azores and that in more recent times hundreds of ships have been forced across the Atlantic by storms and currents. It would not be surprising, they say, if the same had happened to some Roman ships during their voyages along Africa's coast. □

The Shards of Controversy

In 1956, Emilio Estrada, a young Ecuadorian businessman with an interest in the ancient history of his country, began excavating a garbage dump left by the prehistoric residents of the fishing village of Valdivia. Out of the excavation came 36,000 pottery shards, along with numerous artifacts of bone, shell, and stone—and an enduring debate over the meaning of the find.

Estrada himself addressed the problem of origins slowly and carefully. Over a period of several years, he cataloged Valdivia's yield and had the wood and bone fragments carbon-dated. His results showed that the pottery shards were 4,000 to 4,500 years old—at the time, the oldest known pottery in South America. More startling still were the pottery designs. He noted that they were remarkably similar to a style of pottery known as Jomon, which was made during the same ancient period half a world away in Japan.

Estrada concluded that Japanese mariners had sailed to the New World, bringing with them not only their own pots but also pot-making knowledge that was new to the natives. Perhaps the travelers were a band of fishermen, he speculated, blown off course by a Pacific gale. Less likely, they might have been adventurers who set out deliberately to colonize new lands.

No matter how—or if—the Jomon influence arrived, a comparison of Valdivian and Jomon artifacts revealed a remarkable correlation. Experts at the Smithsonian Institution confirmed that twenty-four of the twenty-eight major characteristics of the Valdivian pots were found in Jomon pottery. Their decorative elements and the construction of their spouts were among the most striking of the similarities.

Such resemblances did not, however, settle the matter. Some critics have questioned the accuracy of carbon-dating. Moreover, later excavation in nearby Colombia unearthed pottery that was a thousand years older than the Valdivia finds, casting some doubt on the notion that the Japanese had introduced pottery to Ecuador. Nevertheless, proponents of the Jomon connection cling to their theory and hope that the long-ago garbage dump at Valdivia will one day yield the evidence that will prove them to be right. □

Incised striations on pottery shards from Japan *(far left)* resemble those on shards from Ecuador *(near left)*. Some anthropologists believe the similarity results from transpacific contact between the two cultures in ancient times.

PRE-ANCIENTS

Although it defies the studied findings of historians and archaeologists, the concept is simple enough: Somewhere in the distant past existed civilizations more advanced than those of ancient China, Egypt, Greece, or Rome—and perhaps more advanced even than our own. There are no verifiable chronicles or ruins from those pre-ancient times, the enthusiasts explain, because the wondrous worlds that flourished then were utterly destroyed in a titanic cataclysm. But a handful of lucky survivors escaped the destruction and helped found some of the early civilizations that are known to modern scholarship.

At the heart of this view is the notion that these early civilizations were too brilliant to have leaped into being without guidance and inspiration from the deeper past. Just what the sources of the guidance might have been is not always clear, although some of the more extravagant advocates—such as writer Erich von Däniken—propose that the seeds of pre-ancient earthly civilization were planted by beings from another planet.

Not surprisingly, expert opinion dismisses such beliefs, and proponents are hard put to produce any proofs for their theories. Some point to legends of the lost continent of Atlantis, others to the old and well-nigh universal myths of a pre-ancient existence washed away by a global flood. Still other believers proffer a random array of peculiar signs and curious artifacts—among them a wood-handled metal hammer and a supposed spark plug found encased in apparently solid stone.

Reports of such evidence are fascinating. But without more tangible signs of a pre-ancient world, it is well to acknowledge the fact—almost as marvelous—that the human race as we know it is solely responsible for the climb from primitivism to high civilization.

Map of the Ancient Sea Kings?

In 1929, workers cleaning the Topkapi Palace harem of the last of the Turkish sultans chanced upon a torn and dusty map. It seemed to be a rendering of the coasts of Africa, Spain, and South America. But closer inspection would show it to be more than that. Indeed, it would lead some researchers to claim that ancient seafarers from an unknown civilization discovered Antarctica—and accurately mapped it—thousands of years ago.

Painted on gazelle skin, the map was made in 1513 by a Turkish admiral and one-time pirate named Piri Re'is. No one knows how it disappeared for more than four centuries, but its discovery caused a sensation. What first startled cartographers and historians was an inscription on the map explaining that it was partly based on a chart drawn by Christopher Columbus: "It is reported thus; that a Genoese infidel, his name was Colombo, he it was who discovered these places." There was speculation that the Piri Re'is map might be a link to the fabled Lost Map of Columbus, a chart that the Italian navigator supposedly drew of the West Indies. So thinking, the governments of the United States and Turkey

The Piri Re'is map *(above)* shows part of Africa's west coast and South America's east coast. Some theorists think the southernmost extension of South America at the bottom of the map corresponds to the northwest coast of Antarctica, shown at the bottom of the modern map at left.

began a search for maps related to the sixteenth-century parchment.

They came up empty-handed, and enthusiasm over the map waned, despite important lingering mysteries associated with it. How, for instance, had the map placed Africa and South America at nearly correct longitudes some two centuries before the invention of the chronometer, a precision timepiece modern navigators consider essential for determining longitude? In any case, little was heard of the map for the next twenty-five years or so. Then, in 1956, Arlington Mallery, an archaeologist, engineer, and old-map expert known for propounding the theory that the Vikings reached America before Columbus, studied a copy of it and reached a surprising conclusion.

Mallery claimed that what at first seems to be the extreme southern portion of South America—an area the map depicts as an archipelago stretching southeastward beneath Africa—is actually the bays and islands of Antarctica's northern coast. It has generally been thought that Antarctica's existence was unknown to the world until the 1820s. But if Mallery was right, then someone knew the continent's northern lineaments in the sixteenth century and perhaps—depending on the sources Piri Re'is used to make his map—far earlier.

A hint of just how early the original sources may have been lies in another intriguing feature of the Piri Re'is chart. Geologists believe Antarctica has been buried under ice for two million years. Yet the map appears to include altitudes of mountains now under glaciers. The map's features also correspond dramatically to a 1949 topographical profile of the area, made with seismological equipment. These factors seem to indicate that, somehow, an ancient cartographer mapped at least part of the continent when it was free of ice.

Obviously, no one believes that seafarers visited Antarctica two million years ago. But there is speculation that a much more recent global warming temporarily loosed parts of northern Antarctica from the ice, possibly making it accessible to ancient sailors.

John G. Weihaupt, a University of Colorado specialist in seismology and gravity and planetary geology, is among those holding to this theory. Weihaupt has conducted studies at several antarctic research stations. Along with a number of other geologists, he contends that between 6,000 and 9,000 years ago, the earth was warmer and the glaciers encasing the southernmost continent may have receded for about a thousand years. According to Weihaupt, the melting would have been most likely along Antarctica's western archipelago—the part allegedly shown on the Piri Re'is map.

After reading opinions pro and con about the Piri Re'is map, the scientist questions its authenticity. But he believes certain similarly old maps are authentic and suggest Antarctica may have been known to some seafarers before 1500. Although the original sources used for these Renaissance maps are unknown, Weihaupt says, it is not unthinkable that ancient voyagers trading along the coast of Africa during the global warming thousands of years ago could have gone as far south as Antarctica.

What Weihaupt offers as a tentative theory, another scholar, the late Charles H. Hapgood, asserted as fact. A cartographer and historian at Keene Teachers College in New Hampshire, Hapgood conducted a seven-year investigation of Arlington Mallery's work on the Piri Re'is map. After painstakingly comparing and replotting the topographical features on the Piri Re'is map and other old charts with correspondences on modern maps, the Harvard-trained Hapgood concluded that many geographical features were a close match. In his 1966 book, *Maps of the Ancient Sea Kings: Evidence of Advanced Civilization in the Ice Age,* he wrote that the old maps were "the first hard evidence that advanced peoples preceded all the peoples now known to history." These ancients, Hapgood said, sailed the world pole to pole. "Unbelievable as it may appear," he wrote, "the evidence nevertheless indicates that some ancient people explored the coasts of Antarctica when its coasts were free of ice."

Many experts doubt Mallery's conclusions and deem Hapgood's theory extravagant. Some discount the map's authenticity; others note that even if it is a sixteenth-century chart, Renaissance cartographers often included an "imaginary" southern continent on their maps for symmetry. But if Piri Re'is's Antarctica is a work of the imagination, it seems to be one with an unusual correspondence to reality. Thus controversy about the intriguing parchment continues, and the mystery remains. □

Polar Bearings

Although some scientists doubt the authenticity of the Piri Re'is map *(pages 126-127)*, there is no doubt that another map showing a continent at the South Pole does date from the sixteenth century— some 300 years before the modern discovery of Antarctica. Moreover, this second map *(below)* is more detailed than the Piri Re'is chart, depicting the continent in its entirety and rather closely approximating its correct shape. The map even shows mountain ranges and rivers that, some contend, correspond to those that long ago

vanished beneath glacial ice.

It was devised in 1531 by a Frenchman named Orontius Fineus, a famous cartographer of his day. Fineus carved the world map in the form of a woodcut, and its original prints were bound together in a volume recounting sea voyages. The map's depiction of Antarctica's shape resembles those in modern-day maps, although, when relative scales are adjusted, Fineus's southern continent is much bigger than the real Antarctica, and there are other notable discrepancies. The rotation of the continent in the Fineus map is off by about

twenty degrees, for example, and the long Antarctic Peninsula found on a modern map is absent in the sixteenth-century chart.

Even so, the similarity in shape between Fineus's version and the real Antarctica led historian Charles Hapgood to point to the Fineus map as further proof of his theory that "ancient sea kings," roaming the oceans millennia ago, visited and mapped the polar continent before their civilization mysteriously vanished. Hapgood claimed many correspondences between the old map and modern ones of Antarctica, contending that mountains featured on the Fineus map tally with mountains that have only recently been proved to exist.

His theory has garnered some support. For instance, in 1961, a U.S. Air Force cartographic expert, Captain Lorenzo W. Burroughs, examined the map and vouched for its accuracy. "Beyond a shadow of a doubt," Burroughs said, the Fineus map was "compiled from accurate source maps of Antarctica." By and large, however, the scientific community has discounted Hapgood's assertions. Resemblances between the old map and modern ones, the critics say, are merely coincidences, flukes, the results of lucky guesswork.

According to detractors, Hapgood, though well-intentioned and intellectually honest, was led astray by his enthusiasm for his theory. Cartographic historian David Woodward, a professor of geography at the University of Wisconsin, contends that Hapgood reached his conclusions by vastly overstating similarities between the Fineus map and modern maps and by ignoring discrepancies.

These critics note that the existence of a southern polar continent was widely accepted by sixteenth-century cartographers; indeed, the notion stretched back to antiquity. Many mapmakers of the early Renaissance included a Terra Australis, or "Southern Land," if for no other reason than to give the globe symmetry. In 1520, when the Portuguese navigator Ferdinand Magellan nagivated the strait that now bears his name, most geographers assumed logically—if erroneously—that he had sailed through a

narrow passage separating what is now South America from the long-sought southernmost continent. Thus, at the time Fineus and other cartographers were making their maps, there was fresh support for the polar continent theory.

As to correspondences involving mountains and rivers, critics again contend that Hapgood waxed extravagant in support of his theory. "He didn't realize that unknown coastlines were frequently shown with rivers and headlands," Professor Woodward points out, adding that Hapgood allowed himself considerable geographic license in drawing comparisons between mountains and river channels shown in the Fineus map and actual topographic features that have

been scanned seismologically. And David Jolly, publisher of a handbook for dealers in rare maps, notes that it was common for sixteenth-century cartographers to include in their maps lands more fabled than real and to embellish them not only with rivers and mountains but sometimes even with fictional cities.

Despite these criticisms, Charles Hapgood's theory persists, and the Fineus map continues to intrigue students of cartography. If the likeness between the old woodcut and today's maps is only a coincidence, it is nevertheless a remarkable one. And if Fineus was only guessing when he carved the shape of his polar continent, the guess was uncanny. □

A Rock-Bound Spark Plug

On February 13, 1961, rock hunter Mike Mikesell was working the Coso Mountains near Olancha, California, when he found what he took to be a geode—a hollow stone nodule lined with crystals. But the next day, as he cut the specimen open—ruining a diamond saw blade in the process—he made a singular discovery. His find was not a geode but an ordinary rock—and lodged within it were the apparent remains of a mechanical part, a two-millimeter shaft of porcelain and metal resembling a modern-day spark plug. Mikesell's saw had sliced cleanly through this object.

The Coso artifact, as it soon was called, sparked a continuing controversy. Although the specimen has never been examined closely by independent investigators, the out-

er layer of geological material— sometimes referred to as hardened clay rather than rock—reportedly is peppered with fossil shells and fragments dating to at least 500,000 years ago. This crust is also said to contain two objects resembling a nail and a washer.

Enthusiasts persist in upholding the tantalizing notion that the Coso artifact is a technological remnant of some unknown, long-lost civilization. Critics, noting the numerous abandoned mineshafts in the Coso Mountain area, speculate that the artifact is indeed a spark plug but that it came from an engine used in mining operations. Over the years, they say, the plug became concreted with local mud and fossil debris that took on the appearance of rock. □

A Texas Hammer

During an outing near London, Texas, in June 1934, Emma Hahn and her family came across a rock with a most unusual feature: A fragment of wood was protruding from its surface. Later, after breaking open the rock, the Hahns were surprised to find that the wood was in fact the splintered handle of a hammer—whose well-worn iron head remained intact.

Rock formations in the area where the hammer was found have been reliably dated to the Ordovician geological epoch of nearly a half-billion years ago. The rock encasing the hammer has similar characteristics, leading some enthusiasts to maintain that the tool itself must therefore be an artifact surviving from that distant time.

No part of the implement has been subjected to rigorous testing or dating procedures, however. And most scientists who have considered the case of the rock-bound hammer conclude that it is a result of a natural process of accretion. This occurs when mineral-rich water evaporates, leaving behind deposits that build up until an object becomes completely encased. The process can take place quite quickly: In the Pacific, for example, artifacts from World War II have been found enclosed in rock. The most likely origin of the Texas hammer, it seems, is that it was lost or discarded by a nineteenth-century miner and then encased in material washed from nearby Ordovician rock. □

Atlantean Avenue

For centuries, believers in a great pre-ancient civilization have sought remnants of the lost continent of Atlantis. First described in the fourth century BC by the Greek philosopher Plato—who wrote that his account was based on earlier Egyptian sources—Atlantis is said to have been a huge landmass located somewhere in the Atlantic Ocean. Its inhabitants developed a highly advanced culture and sought to impose their rule on the whole world. Then, some 9,000 years before Plato's time, the entire continent was destroyed by volcanic eruptions and floods.

Many critics, starting with Aristotle, have declared Atlantis a myth concocted by Plato to demonstrate his own political theories. But modern believers have countered that the city of Troy was also deemed a myth until Heinrich Schliemann's discovery in 1873 of a Bronze Age citadel near the Turkish town of Hissarlik. Subsequent excavations have convinced mainstream archaeologists that this was indeed the site of the city-state that inspired the Greek poet Homer's epic work.

Similarly, remnants of Minoan culture on the island of Crete, first excavated in 1900, indicate that this great maritime power was destroyed by a series of cataclysmic volcanic events. This and other parallels have convinced many scholars that garbled tales of the vanished Minoan empire must have been the source of Plato's story about the island of Atlantis.

Opponents of this view agree

that an eruption probably ended Minoan civilization in about 1500 BC but point out that Plato said Atlantis vanished thousands of years before then. Experts explain that this time discrepancy could be the result of a simple error in translation from earlier Egyptian texts; others, though, insist that Plato's chronology is correct and that in any case traces of Atlantis are to be found beyond the Mediterranean—just as Plato declared.

Bolstering this notion are the prognostications of American psychic healer and prophet Edgar Cayce, who died in 1945. Claiming to be in contact with the souls of departed Atlanteans, Cayce predicted that in the late 1960s portions of the lost continent would begin to rise off the coast of the Bahamas. Indeed, in 1968, divers exploring half a mile off the western end of the island of North Bimini discovered a series of intriguing stone slabs lying on the seabed in twenty feet of water. Varying in weight between about one ton and ten tons each, the slabs were arranged in rows, the longest one running along for some 1,600 feet and terminating in a 90 degree bend.

The fitted appearance of the blocks prompted certain enthusiasts to see them as the remains of an ancient wall or road, a view that attracted a number of supporters, among them a Miami zoologist and amateur archaeologist by the name of J. Manson Valentine, who concluded that the arrangement was man-made. Geologists, however, stated that the stones were simply a natural formation of weathered beach rock.

Under the right conditions, they explained, tidal washes of calcium-carbonate-rich seawater can cement together individual grains of sand to form layers of rock in a relatively brief time; temperature extremes and the erosion of sand beneath the formation can then cause regular blocklike fractures. Such formations are not uncommon elsewhere on Bimini and indeed in other parts of the world where there are similar environmental conditions.

Proponents of an arisen Atlantis argued that although the stones may be beach rock, this was merely a convenient local source of building material for the ancients. Moreover, they pointed to the existence of fluted marble columns nearby. But examination of the seabed beneath the columns revealed the remains of a packing crate, along with other debris that indicated a modern-era shipwreck or grounding, a familiar occurrence in those waters. As for the blocks, a series of core samples taken to reveal the characteristics of the stone's internal layers showed that the rocks had not been moved since their natural formation. If there ever was a lost Atlantis, then, it was not located off the shores of Bimini. □

Footprints of the Pre-Ancients

A curious paleontologist from the American Museum of Natural History gave an unwitting boost to the notion of civilizations long predating the scope of modern archaeologists and historians. At the end of a fossil hunting season in the Southwest in 1938, Roland T. Bird was checking a last lead before returning to New York. At a curio shop in Gallup, New Mexico, he examined two thick, flat rocks, each bearing the imprint of a fifteen-inch humanlike foot. The prints were obviously carved fakes (such as the one above), but the store clerk told Bird that some dinosaur tracks, taken from the same locale as the supposed giant human prints, were on display at the owner's other shop in Lupton, Arizona. The reptilian tracks, too, had been recently carved, but they were so anatomically correct that the scientist set out to find the originals from which they had been copied.

His search took him to Glen Rose, Texas. There, firmly imprinted in 100,000,000-year-old rock, he found an abundance of dinosaur tracks. Locals then led him to a ◊

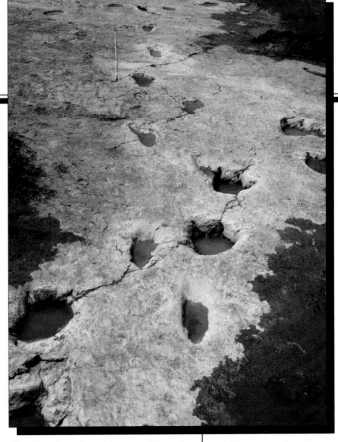

These ancient footprints in a Texas riverbed were once touted as "man tracks," but paleontologists have confirmed that the track makers were dinosaurs, not giant humans.

less distinct print along the Paluxy River. This, they said, was a "man track." Bird at once realized that it was made by a dinosaur. But the print was indistinct and could look human to the untrained eye.

As news of Bird's investigations spread, a garbled version gained currency. It was said that he had found unmistakably human footprints alongside those of a dinosaur. The garbled report was seized upon by numerous enthusiasts, some of whom trekked to Glen Rose and uncovered more of the supposed man tracks—proving, they claimed, that a race of humans walked the earth eons ago. These were the people, said the believers, who raised the advanced civilizations that were destroyed by the cataclysms described in the legends of so many cultures.

Many of the most ardent supporters have long since reexamined and renounced the Glen Rose "man tracks." Others, though, maintain that the area may yet provide proof for their theories. And there are some who buttress their case by citing similar discoveries elsewhere. For example, in 1884, quarry workers near Lake Managua, Nicaragua, found numerous unmistakably human prints in sandstone buried under twelve feet of seemingly ancient strata. At about the same time, humanlike prints were found in a shale stratum at the State Penitentiary in Carson City, Nevada. And, in 1938, prints discovered in 250-million-year-old rock near Berea, Kentucky, looked so human that a local geology professor, Wilbur Burroughs, ascribed them to a creature he dubbed *Phenanthropus mirabilis* (looks human, remarkable).

The scientific community has dismissed such evidence with various explanations. The Nicaraguan footprints, for example, were in a volcanically active area where periodic eruptions, followed by rapid revegetation, could have occurred many times. Hence, the extensive deposition does not necessarily indicate an age greater than the 20,000 years humans are thought to have been in the Americas. The Carson City prints are explained by the fossilized sloth remains found at the same location; sloth prints resemble the human version. And the Berea, Kentucky, footprints were no surprise to anthropologists who had long known of a local Indian tribe that customarily carved such prints along with other figures used in their religion. Still other human-footprint-like features have been ascribed to ancient animal and insect burrows and the random effects of erosion on different forms of rock. □

Some Curious Finds

The belief that advanced human civilizations flourished during prehistoric times stretches back at least to the nineteenth century. So, too, does a record of singular archaeological finds that are often cited to support the possibility. However, it is impossible to examine any of the physical evidence: None of the alleged artifacts or remains has survived to the present time.

Similarly, although many of the reports appear to have been gathered by earnest and dependable witnesses, even accounts by scientific authorities are suspect. Geology and paleontology were young sciences at the time, still lacking a comprehensive body of theory to explain rock formation and develop reliable dating techniques. And the possibility of fraud or hoax cannot be ruled out. Whatever the underlying truth may be, the volume and the variety of these reports make for an intriguing catalog of antiquarian lore:

- In his *Fossils of the South Downs,* published in 1822, British surgeon and amateur geologist Gideon Mantell chronicled a number of anomalous finds, including references to other works. For example, he noted the 1791 account of an M. Leisky of Hamburg, Germany, who fractured a piece of flint and discovered an "ancient brass pin" in the center. Mantell also mentioned the discovery of 126 silver coins enclosed in flints at Grinoe, Denmark.

- In 1831, *The American Journal of Science and Arts* reported a curious find in a marble quarry some twelve miles northwest of Philadelphia. While cutting a thirty-cubic-foot slab, workers found a 1½ by ⅝ inch indentation in the stone. In the center of this were two raised symbols resembling the letters *NI.*

- On Christmas Eve, 1851, the *Times* of London reported the case of a miner who was returning from the California gold fields with a large block of gold-bearing quartz. After accidentally dropping and breaking his sample, the man discovered an iron nail embedded near its center.

- In June 1852, *Scientific American* appealed to its readership for help in solving a puzzling discovery near Dorchester, Massachusetts, the year before. After blasting a formation of pudding stone, workers found two halves of a bell-shaped vessel. Described as 4½ inches high by 6½ inches at the base and 2½ inches at the top, the object, adorned with silver inlaid flowers, baffled local antiquarians. One speculation was that the article was the bowl of an East Indian water pipe lost in the soil near the blast by one of the sea captains known to have lived in the neighborhood.

- In 1853, the Cusick's Mill quarry, near Zanesville, Ohio, yielded the bones of a woman completely entombed in sandstone that also retained the full impression of her once fleshly form. The Zanesville *Courier* also reported an adjacent cavity that had been molded from a pair of human hands.

- James Parsons and his two sons were mining coal at a strip mine in Hammondsville, Ohio, in the autumn of 1868 when a barrier of coal collapsed, revealing a smooth slate wall said to contain twenty-five hieroglyphic characters carved in bold relief. Scholars could not identify the meaning or origin of the symbols.

- During the winter of 1869, the Miner's Saloon in Treasure City, Nevada, exhibited a piece of feldspar containing a two-inch screw, a specimen lately unearthed from the local Abbey Mine.

- In 1877, crowds in Eureka, Nevada, thrilled to a discovery made in the adjacent hills. There, prospectors had found the bones of a supposedly human leg partly embedded in quartzite. Measuring thirty-nine inches from just above the knees to the tip of the toe, the remains indicated a person of extraordinary stature.

- J. Q. Adams, writing in the May 1883 issue of *American Antiquarian,* reported the discovery of a thimble trapped in a lump of lignite mined from the Marshal Coal Bed in Colorado.

- In June 1891, Mrs. S. W. Culp of Morrisonville, Illinois, was surprised to find a ten-inch gold chain embedded in a lump of coal she was breaking apart for her stove. The local newspaper described the event as "a study for the students of archaeology who love to puzzle their brains over the geological construction of the earth from whose ancient depths the curious is always cropping out." □

ACKNOWLEDGMENTS

The editors wish to thank these individuals and institutions for their valuable assistance in the preparation of this volume:

Jan Amnehäl, Göteborgs Stad Etnografiska Museet, Gothenburg, Sweden; Ferdinand Anton, Munich; François Avril, Conservateur au Département des Manuscrits, Bibliothèque Nationale, Paris; Brigitte Baumbusch, Scala, Florence, Italy; Robert S. Bianchi, The Brooklyn Museum, New York; Allan G. Bromley, University of Sydney, Australia; D. R. Brothwell, Institute of Archaeology, London; Onno Brouwer, University of Wisconsin, Madison; Edmund Buchner, Kommission für Alte Geschichte und Epigraphik, Munich; Carol R. Butler, Smithsonian Institution, Washington, D.C.; Ron Calais, Lafayette, La.; Jeff Chester, National Air and Space Museum, Washington, D.C.; Cathy Crandal, Washington University, St. Louis, Mo.; Edward M. Croom, Jr., University of Mississippi, University; Simmi Dhanda, New Delhi, India; Anna Maria Donadoni, Museo delle Antichità Egizie, Turin, Italy; James A. Duke, Department of Agriculture, Beltsville, Md.; Arne Eggebrecht, Roemer und Pelizaeus Museum, Hildesheim, West Germany; Clark L. Erickson, University of Pennsylvania, Philadelphia; Judith Fields, The Science Museum, London; Ben R. Finney, University of Hawaii, Honolulu; Christian Fischer, Silkeborg Museum, Denmark; Kenneth Franklin, Port Angeles, Washington; Tim Fraser, London; diya' Abou Ghazi, The Egyptian Antiquities Organization, Cairo; William H. Gotwald, Jr., Utica College, New York; Klaus Grewe, Volker Dünnhaupt, Rheinisches Landesmuseum, Bonn; Joel Grossman, Grossman and Associates, New York; Mark Hall, University of California, Berkeley; Ann Harmon, Laytonsville, Md.; James A. Harrell, University of Toledo, Ohio; Michael R. Harris, Smithsonian Institution, Washington, D.C.; Lothar Haselberger, Kommission für Alte Geschichte und Epigraphik, Munich; Barbara Hicks, London; Whitney Hodges, Washington University, St. Louis, Mo.; H. T. Huang, The Needham Research Institute, Cambridge, England; Lynn H. Hutto, Biopharm U.S.A., Charleston, S.C.; Istituto Archeologico Germanico, Rome; Peter L. Jakab, National Air and Space Museum, Washington, D.C.; Michael Jansen, Forschungsprojekt Mohenjo-Daro, Aachen, West Germany; Boma Johnson, U.S. Department of the Interior, Yuma, Ariz.; Charalambos Karakalos, Hellenic Atomic Energy Committee, Athens; Ivan Katic, The Royal Danish Veterinary and Agricultural Library, Copenhagen; Kay Kavanagh, Brussels; David H. Kelley, Calgary, Alberta; Bob Kiener, Washington, D.C.; Mette Korsholm, The National Museum of Denmark, Copenhagen; Glen J. Kuban, North Royalton, Ohio; Georgia Lee, UCLA Archaeology Department, Los Osos, Calif.; Walter H. Lewis, Washington University, St. Louis, Mo.; Liang Lien-Chu, The Needham Research Institute, Cambridge, England; Michael H. Logan, University of Tennessee, Knoxville; Sue Lundene, Runestone Museum, Alexandria, Minn.; Ewan Mackie, The Hunterian Museum, Glasgow, Scotland; Adel Mahmoud, The Egyptian Museum, Cairo; Michael Marshall, Corales, N.Mex.; Khalil Messiha, Cairo University; Mohammad Mohsen, The Egyptian Museum, Cairo; Robert Montgomery, National Museum of Health and Medicine, Washington, D.C.; William Morgan, Jacksonville, Fla.; Musée Gaumais, Virton, Luxembourg; Joseph Needham, The Needham Research Institute, Cambridge, England; Dr. Larry S. Nichter, Children's Hospital of Los Angeles, Calif.; Charles Ortloff, FMC Corporation, Santa Clara, Calif.; Emmerich Pasztory, Hoechst AG., Frankfurt; Gena F. Paulk, Rock Eagle 4-H Center, Eastonton, Ga.; Margaret Ponting, Callanish, Scotland; Dories Reents-Budet, Duke University, Durham, N.C.; Luisa Ricciarini, Milan; Ed E. Richardson, Dumbarton Oaks, Washington, D.C.; Rudy Rosenburg, Leeches U.S.A., Westbury, N.Y.; Colette Roubet, Directeur du Museum d'Histoire Naturelle, Paris; Jean-Loup Rousselot, Museum für Völkerkunde, Munich; Roy T. Sawyer, Biopharm (U.K.) Ltd., Hendy, South Wales; Denise Schmandt-Besserat, University of Texas, Austin; William A. Shear, Hampton-Sydney College, Va.; Nathan Sivin, University of Pennsylvania, Philadelphia; Duncan Spencer, Washington, D.C.; Warren E. Steiner, Smithsonian Institution, Washington, D.C.; Sayyed Tawfig, The Egyptian Antiquities Organization, Cairo; Allen Thrasher, Library of Congress, Washington, D.C.; Paul Tolstoy, University of Montreal, Canada; Lindley Vann, University of Maryland, College Park; John W. Verano, Smithsonian Institution, Washington, D.C.; Jay Von Werlhof, Imperial Valley College Museum, Centro, Calif.; Jeffrey Wadsworth, Lockheed Missiles and Space Company, Palo Alto, Calif.; John G. Weihaupt, University of Colorado, Denver; Wilfried Werner, Universitätsbibliothek, Handschriftenabteilung, Heidelberg, West Germany; Stephen Williams, Harvard University, Cambridge, Mass.; Bonnie Winslow, Bloomfield, N.Mex.; David Woodward, University of Wisconsin, Madison.

BIBLIOGRAPHY

Books

Ackerknecht, Erwin H., M.D. *A Short History of Medicine.* Baltimore: Johns Hopkins University Press, 1982.

Aikman, Lonnelle. *Nature's Healing Arts: From Folk Medicine to Modern Drugs.* Washington, D.C.: National Geographic Society, 1977.

Alcina Franch, José. *Pre-Columbian Art.* Translated by I. Mark Paris. New York: Harry N. Abrams, 1983.

Ascher, Marcia, and Robert Ascher. *Code of the Quipu.* Ann Arbor: University of Michigan Press, 1981.

Ashe, Geoffrey, et al. *The Quest for America.* New York: Praeger Publishers, 1971.

Asimov, Isaac. *Asimov's Biographical Encyclopedia of Science and Technology.* Garden City, N.Y.: Doubleday, 1964.

Auguet, Roland. *The Roman Games.* St. Albans, Hertfordshire, England: Panther Books, 1975.

Aveni, Anthony F. *Skywatchers of Ancient Mexico.* Austin: University of Texas Press, 1980.

Baines, John and Jaromír Málek. *Atlas of Ancient Egypt.* New York: Facts on File Publications, 1980.

Benét, William Rose. *The Reader's Encyclopedia* (2nd ed.). New York: Thomas Y. Crowell, 1965.

Berkow, Robert, M.D. (Ed.). *The Merck Manual of Diagnosis and Therapy,* (14th ed.). Rahway, N.J.: Merck Sharp & Dohme Research Laboratories, 1982.

Berlitz, Charles. *Mysteries from Forgotten Worlds.* Garden City, N.Y.: Doubleday, 1972.

Blunden, Caroline, and Mark Elvin. *Cultural Atlas of China.* Oxford: Phaidon Press, 1983.

Bord, Janet. *Mazes and Labyrinths of the World.* New York: E. P. Dutton, 1976.

Bord, Janet, and Colin Bord:
Ancient Mysteries of Britain. Manchester, N.H.: Salem House, 1986.
Mysterious Britain. New York: Granada Publishing, 1974.

Brecher, Kenneth, and Michael Feirtag (Eds.).

Astronomy of the Ancients. Cambridge, Mass.: MIT Press, 1979.

Brennan, Martin. *The Stars and the Stones: Ancient Art and Astronomy in Ireland.* London: Thames & Hudson, 1983.

Brooksmith, Peter (Ed.). *The Unexplained: Mysteries of Mind, Space and Time* (Vol. 7). New York: Marshall Cavendish, 1986.

Builders of the Ancient World: Marvels of Engineering. Washington, D.C.: Special Publications Division, National Geographic Society, 1986.

Burton, David M. *The History of Mathematics: An Introduction.* Newton, Mass.: Allyn & Bacon, 1985.

Calder, Nigel. *Timescale.* New York: Viking Press, 1983.

Canby, Courtlandt. *The Past Displayed: A Journey through the Ancient World.* Oxford: Phaidon Press, 1980.

Carcopino, Jérôme. *Daily Life in Ancient Rome.* Edited by Henry T. Rowell, translated by E. O. Lorimer. New Haven: Yale University Press, 1940.

Casson, Lionel, et al. *Mysteries of the Past.* Edited by Joseph J. Thorndike, Jr. New York: American Heritage, 1977.

Castleden, Rodney. *The Wilmington Giant: The Quest for a Lost Myth.* Wellingborough, Northamptonshire, England: Turnstone Press, 1983.

Cavendish, Richard:
Mysteries of the Universe. New York: Galahad Books, 1981.
Prehistoric England. New York: British Heritage Press, 1983.

Cazeau, Charles J., and Stuart D. Scott, Jr. *Exploring the Unknown: Great Mysteries Reexamined.* New York: Plenum Press, 1979.

Charroux, Robert. *Forgotten Worlds.* Translated by Lowell Bair. New York: Walker, 1973.

Childress, David Hatcher. *Lost Cities of Ancient Lemuria & the Pacific.* Stelle, Ill.: Adventures Unlimited Press, 1988.

Chippindale, Christopher. *Stonehenge Complete.* New York: Thames & Hudson, 1983.

Closs, Michael P. (Ed.). *Native American Mathematics.* Austin: University of Texas Press, 1986.

Coe, Michael, Dean Snow, and Elizabeth Benson. *Altas of Ancient America.* New York: Facts on File Publications, 1986.

Cohen, Daniel. *The Encyclopedia of the Strange.* New York: Dodd, Mead & Co., 1985.

Corliss, William R. (Comp.). *Ancient Man: A Handbook of Puzzling Artifacts.* Glen Arm, Md.: Sourcebook Project, 1978.

Cornell, Tim, and John Matthews. *Atlas of the Roman World.* Oxford: Phaidon Press, 1982.

De Camp, L. Sprague, and Catherine C. De Camp.

Ancient Ruins and Archaeology. Garden City, N.Y.: Doubleday, 1964.

Durán, Fray Diego. *Book of the Gods and Rites and the Ancient Calendar.* Edited and translated by Fernando Horcasitas and Doris Heyden. Norman: University of Oklahoma Press, 1971.

Empires Ascendant (TimeFrame series). Alexandria, Va.: Time-Life Books, 1987.

Facts & Fallacies. Pleasantville, N.Y.: Reader's Digest Association, 1988.

Fischer, Steven Roger. *Evidence for Hellenic Dialect in the Phaistos Disk.* Berne, Switzerland: Peter Lang, 1988.

Fisher, Douglas Alan. *The Epic of Steel.* New York: Harper & Row, 1963.

Forbes, R. J. *Man the Maker.* New York: Abelard-Schuman, 1958.

Fraser, Peter Marshall. *Ptolemaic Alexandria.* London: Oxford University Press, 1972.

Fu Tianchou. *Wonders from the Earth: The First Emperor's Underground Army.* San Francisco: China Books and Periodicals, 1989.

Garvin, Richard M. *The Crystal Skull.* Garden City, N.Y.: Doubleday, 1973.

Gibbs-Smith, Charles H. *A History of Flying.* London: B. T. Batsford, 1953.

Gordon, Cyrus H. *Riddles in History.* New York: Crown Publishers, 1974.

Grant, Michael. *The Etruscans.* New York: Charles Scribner's Sons, 1980.

Gray, Randal, Susan Hill, and Robin L. K. Wood (Eds.). *Lost Worlds: Alastair Service.* London: Collins, 1981.

Hadingham, Evan. *Early Man and the Cosmos.* New York: Walker Publishing Co., 1984.

Haining, Peter. *Ancient Mysteries.* New York: Taplinger Publishing Co., 1977.

Hall, Robert A., Jr. *The Kensington Rune-Stone Is Genuine: Linguistic, Practical, Methodological Considerations.* Columbia, S.C.: Hornbeam Press, 1982.

Hapgood, Charles H. *Maps of the Ancient Sea Kings: Evidence of Advanced Civilization in the Ice Age.* New York: Chilton Books, 1966.

Harris, Harold A. *Sport in Greece and Rome.* London: Thames & Hudson, 1972.

Hart, Olive:
The Dream of Flight. New York: Winchester Press, 1972.
The Prehistory of Flight. Berkeley: University of California Press, 1985.

Hawkins, Gerald S., with John B. White. *Stonehenge Decoded.* Garden City, N.Y.: Doubleday, 1965.

Hellemans, Alexander, and Bryan Bunch. *The Timetables of Science.* New York: Simon & Schuster, 1988.

Hitching, Francis. *The Mysterious World: An*

Atlas of the Unexplained. New York.: Holt, Reinhart & Winston, 1979.

Hyde, Walter Woodburn. *Ancient Greek Mariners.* New York: Oxford University Press, 1947.

Ifrah, Georges. *From One to Zero: A Universal History of Numbers.* Translated by Lowell Bair. New York: Viking Penguin, 1985.

Jackson, Ralph. *Doctors and Diseases in the Roman Empire.* Norman: University of Oklahoma Press, 1988.

Jones, Henry Stuart. *Companion to Roman History.* Oxford: Clarendon Press, 1912.

Katz, Friedrich. *The Ancient American Civilizations.* Translated by K. M. Lois Simpson. New York: Praeger Publishers, 1972.

Keuneman, Herbert. *Sri Lanka.* Edited by John Gottberg Anderson. Hong Kong: APA Productions, 1984.

Kincaid, Chris (Ed.). *Chaco Roads Project Phase 1.* Albuquerque, N.Mex.: Department of the Interior, Bureau of Land Management, 1983.

Kramer, Samuel Noah. *History Begins at Sumer: Thirty-Nine Firsts in Man's Recorded History.* Philadelphia: University of Pennsylvania Press, 1981.

Kreig, Margaret B. *Green Medicine: The Search for Plants that Heal . . . .* Chicago: Rand McNally, 1964.

Krupp, E. C. (Ed.):
Echoes of the Ancient Skies. New York: Harper & Row, 1983.
In Search of Ancient Astronomies. New York: McGraw-Hill, 1978.

Kumar Das, Sri Surendra. *Ramayana.* Orissa, India: Panchali Publications, 1977.

Laufer, Berthold. *The Prehistory of Aviation* (Studies in Culture History series). Chicago: Chicago Natural History Museum, 1928.

Leonard, Jonathan Norton, and the Editors of Time-Life Books. *Ancient America* (Great Ages of Man series). New York: Time Incorporated, 1967.

Lewis, David. *We, the Navigators.* Canberra: Australian National University Press, 1972.

Leyenaar, Ted J. J., and Lee A. Parsons. *Ulama: The Ballgame of the Mayas and Aztecs.* Leiden, The Netherlands: Spruyt, Van Mantgem & De Does, 1988.

Lisowski, F. P. "Prehistoric and Early Historic Trepanation." In *Diseases in Antiquity,* edited and compiled by Don Brothwell and A. T. Sandison. Springfield, Ill.: Charles C Thomas, 1967.

Lyons, Albert S., M.D., and R. Joseph Petrucelli II, M.D. *Medicine: An Illustrated History.* New York: Harry N. Abrams, 1978.

Lyttle, Richard B. *The Games They Played: Sports in History.* New York: Atheneum, 1982.

McKern, Sharon S. *Exploring the Unknown: Mysteries in American Archaeology.* New York: Praeger Publishers, 1972.

McMann, Jean. *Riddles of the Stone Age: Rock Carvings of Ancient Europe.* London: Thames & Hudson, 1980.

Magic and Medicine of Plants. Pleasantville, N.Y.: Reader's Digest Association, 1986.

Majno, Guido. *The Healing Hand: Man and Wound in the Ancient World.* Cambridge, Mass.: Harvard University Press, 1975.

Margetts, Edward L. "Trepanation of the Skull by the Medicine-Men of Primitive Cultures." In *Diseases in Antiquity,* edited and compiled by Don Brothwell and A. T. Sandison. Springfield, Ill.: Charles C Thomas, 1967.

Marshack, Alexander. *The Roots of Civilization: The Cognitive Beginnings of Man's First Art, Symbol and Notation.* New York: McGraw-Hill, 1972.

Matthews, William Henry. *Mazes and Labyrinths.* Detroit: Singing Tree Press, Book Tower, 1969 (original publication, 1922).

Mayr, Otto (Ed.). *Philosophers and Machines.* New York: Science History Publications, 1976.

Menninger, Karl. *Number Words and Number Symbols: A Cultural History of Numbers.* Translated by Paul Broneer. Cambridge, Mass.: MIT Press, 1969.

Michell, John. *Megalithomania.* Ithaca, New York: Cornell University Press, 1982.

Michell, John, and Robert J. M. Rickard. *Phenomena: A Book of Wonders.* London: Thames & Hudson, 1977.

Moffatt, Michael. *The Origins* (Vol. 1 of *The Ages of Mathematics*). Garden City, N.Y.: Doubleday, 1977.

Morley, Sylvanus Griswold, and George W. Brainerd. *The Ancient Maya* (4th ed.). Revised by Robert J. Sharer. Stanford: Stanford University Press, 1983.

Morley, Sylvanus Griswold, and J. Eric S. Thompson. *An Introduction to the Study of the Maya Hieroglyphs.* New York: Dover Publications, 1975.

Moscati, Sabatino. *The Phoenicians.* New York: Abbeville Press, 1988.

Mysteries of the Ancient Americas. Pleasantville, N.Y.: Reader's Digest Association, 1986.

Mystic Places (Mysteries of the Unknown series). Alexandria, Va.: Time-Life Books, 1987.

Needham, Joseph:

Clerks and Craftsmen in China and the West. Cambridge, England: Cambridge University Press, 1970.

Science and Civilisation in China (Vols. 3 & 4). Cambridge, England: Cambridge University Press, 1959.

Trans-Pacific Echoes and Resonances; Listening Once Again. Philadelphia: World Scientific Publishing Co., 1985.

Neugebauer, O. *The Exact Sciences in Antiquity.* Providence, R.I.: Brown University Press, 1957.

Nickell, Joe, with John F. Fischer. *Secrets of the Supernatural: Investigating the World's Occult Mysteries.* Buffalo, N.Y.: Prometheus Books, 1988.

Noorbergen, René. *Secrets of the Lost Races.* New York: The Bobbs-Merrill Co., 1977.

Nordenskiöld, Erland. *Modifications in Indian Culture through Inventions and Loans.* Gothenburg, Sweden: Elanders Boktryckeri Aktiebolag, 1930.

O'Kelly, Michael J. *Newgrange: Archaeology, Art and Legend.* London: Thames & Hudson, 1982.

Palmer, Martin (Ed.). *T'ung Shu: The Ancient Chinese Almanac.* Translated by Martin Palmer with Mak Hin Chung, Kwok Man Ho, and Angela Smith. Boston: Shambhala, 1986.

Parsons, Edward Alexander. *The Alexandrian Library: Glory of the Hellenic World.* New York: Elsevier Press, 1952.

Piggott, Stuart. *The Earliest Wheeled Transport: From the Atlantic Coast to the Caspian Sea.* London: Thames & Hudson, 1983.

Pomerance, Leon. *The Phaistos Disc: An Interpretation of Astronomical Symbols.* Gothenburg, Sweden: Paul Åströms Förlag, 1976.

Ponting, Gerald, and Margaret Ponting. *New Light on the Stones of Callanish.* Callanish, Isle of Lewis: G & M Ponting, 1984.

Prideaux, Tom, and the Editors of Time-Life Books. *Cro-Magnon Man* (The Emergence of Man series). Alexandria, Va.: Time-Life Books, 1973.

Quest for the Past. Pleasantville, N.Y.: Reader's Digest Association, 1984.

Ragette, Friedrich. *Baalbek.* Park Ridge, N.J.: Noyes Press, 1980.

Raschke, Wendy J. (Ed.). *The Archaeology of the Olympics: The Olympics and Other Festivals in Antiquity.* Madison, Wis.: University of Wisconsin Press, 1988.

Renfrew, Colin. *Before Civilization: The Radiocarbon Revolution and Prehistoric Europe.* New York: Alfred A. Knopf, 1973.

Riley, Carroll L., et al. (Eds.). *Man across the Sea: Problems of Pre-Columbian Contacts.* Austin: University of Texas Press, 1971.

Robinson, David M. *Baalbek Palmyra.* New York: J. J. Augustin Publishers, 1946.

Ronan, Colin A. *Lost Discoveries.* New York: McGraw-Hill, 1973.

Sagan, Carl. *Cosmos.* New York: Random House, 1980.

Sanderson, Ivan T. *Investigating the Unexplained: A Compendium of Disquieting Mysteries of the Natural World.* Englewood Cliffs, N.J.: Prentice-Hall, 1972.

Saunders, E. Dale. *Mudra: A Study of Symbolic Gestures in Japanese Buddhist Sculpture.* New York: Pantheon Books, 1960.

Schele, Linda, and Mary Ellen Miller. *The Blood of Kings: Dynasty and Ritual in Maya Art.* Fort Worth, Tex.: Kimbell Art Museum, 1986.

Service, Alastair. *Lost Worlds.* London: Collins, 1981.

Shao, Paul. *Asiatic Influences in Pre-Columbian American Art.* Ames: Iowa State University Press, 1976.

Shirley, Rodney W. *The Mapping of the World: Early Printed World Maps, 1472-1700.* London: Holland Press, 1984.

Singer, Charles, et al. (Eds.). *The Mediterranean Civilizations and the Middle Ages, c. 700 B.C. to c. A.D. 1500* (Vol. 2 of *A History of Technology*). London: Oxford University Press, 1956.

Smith, J. Russell. *The Story of Iron and Steel.* New York: D. Appleton and Co., 1908.

Smith, William, William Wayte, and G. E. Marindin (Eds.). *A Dictionary of Greek and Roman Antiquities* (Vol. I). London: John Murray, 1914.

Stefansson, Vilhjalmur. *Beyond the Pillars of Heracles: The Classical World Seen through the Eyes of Its Discoverers.* Edited by Evelyn Stefansson Nef. New York: Delacorte Press, 1966.

Strange Stories, Amazing Facts. Pleasantville, N.Y.: Reader's Digest Association, 1981.

Sullivan, John W. W. *The Story of Metals.* Cleveland, Ohio: American Society for Metals; Ames: Iowa State College Press, 1951.

Swaddling, Judith. *The Ancient Olympic Games.* London: British Museum Publication, 1980.

Taton, René (Ed.). *Ancient and Medieval Science* (Vol. 1 of History of Science). Translated by A. J. Pomerans. New York: Basic Books, 1963.

Temple, Robert K. G. *China: Land of Discovery.* Wellingborough, Northamptonshire, England: Patrick Stephens, 1986.

Thorndike, Joseph J., Jr. (Ed.). *Discovery of Lost Worlds.* New York: American Heritage Publishing Co., 1979.

Thorwald, Jürgen. *Science and Secrets of Early Medicine.* Translated by Richard Winston and Clara Winston. New York: Harcourt, Brace & World, 1963.

Throckmorton, Peter (Ed.). *The Sea Remembers: Shipwrecks and Archaeology.* New York: Weidenfeld & Nicolson, 1987.

Tomas, Andrew. *We Are Not the First: Riddles of*

Ancient Science. London: Souvenir Press, 1971.

Veer, M. H. J. Th. van der, and P. Moerman. *Hidden Worlds: Fresh Clues to the Past.* London: Souvenir Press, 1974.

Von Hagen, Victor W. *The Desert Kingdoms of Peru.* Greenwich, Conn.: New York Graphic Society Publishers, 1965.

Welfare, Simon and John Fairley. *Arthur C Clarke's Mysterious World.* New York: A & W Publishers, 1980.

Wernick, Robert, and the Editors of Time-Life Books. *The Monument Builders* (The Emergence of Man series). New York: Time-Life Books, 1973.

White, K. D. *Greek and Roman Technology.* London: Thames & Hudson, 1984.

White, Randall. *Dark Caves, Bright Visions: Life in Ice Age Europe.* New York: American Museum of Natural History, in association with W. W. Norton & Co., 1986.

Williamson, Ray A. (Ed.). *Archaeoastronomy in the Americas.* Los Altos, Calif.: Ballena Press, 1981.

Woolf, Harry (Ed.). *The Analytic Spirit.* Ithaca, New York: Cornell University Press, 1981.

The World Almanac Book of the Strange. New York: New American Library, 1977.

The World's Last Mysteries. Pleasantville, N.Y.: Reader's Digest Association, 1977.

Zaslavsky, Claudia. *Africa Counts.* Boston: Prindle, Weber & Schmidt, 1973.

Zhongmin, Han, and Hubert Delahaye. *A Journey through Ancient China.* New York: Gallery Books, 1985.

PERIODICALS

Abercrombie, Thomas J. "Young-Old Lebanon Lives by Trade." *National Geographic,* April 1958.

"African Presence in Early America." *Journal of African Civilizations* (New Brunswick, N.J.), 1987.

Agogino, George A. "The Crystal Skull: Fine Fake or Authentic Artifact?" *Pursuit,* 1982, Vol. 15, no. 3.

Aikman, Lonnelle. "Nature's Gifts to Medicine." *National Geographic,* September 1974.

Aufderheide, Arthur C., M.D. "The Enigma of Ancient Cranial Trepanation." *Minnesota Medicine,* February 1985.

Bergman, Arieh, et al. "Acceleration of Wound Healing by Topical Application of Honey: An Animal Model." *American Journal of Surgery,* March 1983.

Bird, Roland T. "Thunder in His Footsteps." *Natural History,* May 1939.

Bliquez, Lawrence J. "Classical Prosthetics." *Archaeology,* September/October 1983.

"Bloodsuckers from France." *Time,* December 14, 1981.

Browman, David L. "New Light on Andean Tiwanaku." *American Scientist,* 1981, Vol. 69, pp. 408-419.

Brown, Raymond Lamont. "Medicine and Magic in Ancient Eqypt." *History of Medicine,* Autumn 1972.

Cahill, T. A. "The Vinland Map, Revisited: New Compositional Evidence on Its Inks and Parchment." *Analytical Chemistry,* March 15, 1987.

Carlson, John B. "Pre-Columbian Voyages to the New World: An Overiew." *Early Man,* Spring 1980.

Carter, George F. "Fu-Sang: China Discovers America." *Oceans,* May 1978.

Civil, Miguel. "The Invention of Writing." *Humanities,* October 1986.

Colimore, Edward. "In Peru, Unearthing Ancient Farm Methods." *Philadelphia Inquirer,* March 31, 1989.

Conniff, Richard. "The Little Suckers Have Made a Comeback." *Discover,* August 1987.

Cooper, Chris. "Ancient Technology: A Catalogue of Curious Finds." *The Unexplained: Mysteries of Mind, Space & Time* (London), Orbis, 1981.

Cross, Frank Moore, Jr. "The Pheonician Inscription from Brazil: A Nineteenth-Century Forgery." *Orientacia,* 1968, Vol. 37, no. 4.

Dam, Laura van. "Old Lore, New Cure." *Technology Review,* October 1986.

Daniel, Glyn. "The Minnesota Petroglyph." *Antiquity,* 1958.

D'Errico, Francesco. "Palaeolithic Lunar Calendars: A Case of Wishful Thinking?" *Current Anthropology,* 1989, Vol. 30, no. 1.

DeWitt, David A. "The Water-Powered Pyramid." *Pursuit,* 1984, Vol. 17, no. 1.

Efem, S. E. E. "Clinical Observations on the Wound Healing Properties of Honey." *British Journal of Surgery,* July 1988.

Eisner, T., and H. E. Eisner. "Mystery of a Millipede." *Natural History,* March 1965.

Epstein, Jeremiah F. "Pre-Columbian Old World Coins in America: An Examination of the Evidence." *Current Anthropology,* February 1980.

Erickson, Clark L. "Raised Field Agriculture in the Lake Titicaca Basin." *Expedition* (The University Museum), 1989, Vol. 30, no. 3.

"From Reckoning to Writing." *Scientific American,* August 1975.

Godfrey, Laurie R., and John R. Cole. "Blunder in Their Footsteps." *Natural History,* August 1986.

Gray, Willard F. M. "A Shocking Discovery." *Journal of the Electrochemical Society,* September 1963.

Greenwood, Stuart W. "Golden Models of An-cient Spacecraft?" *Info Journal,* January 1977.

Habeck, Reinhard. "Electricity in Ancient Times." Translated by Ulrich Magin. *Pursuit,* 1985, Vol. 18, no. 1.

Hamblin, Dora Jane. "Unlocking the Secrets of the Giza Plateau." *Smithsonian,* April 1986.

Hathaway, Bruce. "The Ancient Canal That Turned Uphill." *Science 82,* October 1982.

Hencken, Hugh O'Neill. "What Are Pattee's Caves?" *Scientific American,* 1940, Vol. 163, pp. 258-259.

Hitching, Francis. "Sirius B.: Memories of a Distant Star?" *The Unexplained: Mysteries of Mind, Space & Time,* (London), Orbis, 1980.

Hood, M. S. F. "The Tartaria Tablets." *Antiquity,* 1967, Vol. 41, pp. 99-113.

Jett, Stephen C. "The Development and Distribution of the Blowgun." *Annals of the Association of American Geographers,* December 1970.

Jolly, David C. "Was Antarctica Mapped by the Ancients?" *Skeptical Inquirer,* Fall 1986.

Kolata, Alan L. "Tiwanaku and Its Hinterland." *Archaeology,* January/February 1987.

Lechtman, Heather. "Pre-Columbian Surface Metallurgy." *Scientific American,* June 1984.

Lieberman, Stephen J. "Of Clay Pebbles, Hollow Clay Balls, and Writing: A Sumerian View." *American Journal of Archaeology,* July 1980.

Lothrop, Eleanor. "Mystery of the Prehistoric Stone Balls." *Natural History,* September 1955.

McCulloch, J. Huston. "The Bat Creek Inscription: Cherokee Or Hebrew?" *Tennessee Anthropologist,* Fall 1988.

McEwan, Gordon F., and D. Bruce Dickson. "Valdivia, Jomon Fishermen, and the Nature of the North Pacific . . . . ." *American Antiquity,* 1978, Vol. 43, pp. 362-371.

Mahan, Joseph B., Jr. "The Bat Creek Stone." *Tennessee Archaeologist,* February 1973.

Mapes, Glynn. "In Swansea, Wales, There's a Sucker Born Every Minute." *The Wall Street Journal,* September 21, 1989.

Marshack, Alexander:
"Exploring the Mind of Ice Age Man." *National Geographic,* January 1975.
"An Ice Age Ancestor?" *National Geographic,* October 1988.
"Ice Age Art." *Symbols,* Winter 1981.

Maryon, Herbert. "A Note on Magic Mirrors." *Archives of the Chinese Art Society of America,* 1963, Vol. 17.

Meggers, Betty J. "Did Japanese Fishermen Really Reach Ecuador 5,000 Years Ago?" *Early Man,* 1980, Vol. 2, pp. 15-19.

Mendelssohn, Kurt. "A Scientist Looks at the Pyramids."*American Scientist,* 1971, Vol. 59, pp. 210-220.

Mullen, William. "An Empire to Rival Rome, Part II." *Fate,* August 1988.

Murray, Julia K., and Suzanne E. Cahill. "Recent Advances in Understanding the Mystery of Ancient Chinese 'Magic Mirrors.' " *Chinese Science,* 1987, Vol. 8.

Neustupny, Evzen. "The Tartaria Tablets: A Chronological Issue." *Antiquity,* 1968, Vol. 42, pp. 32-35.

Nichter, Larry S., Raymond F. Morgan, and Mark A. Nichter, "The Impact of Indian Methods for Total Nasal Reconstruction." *Clinics in Plastic Surgery,* October 1983.

"A $1 Million Forgery?" *Time,* February 4, 1974.

Ortloff, Charles R. "Canal Builders of Pre-Inca Peru." *Scientific American,* December 1988.

Park, Chris C. "Water Resources and Irrigation Agriculture in Pre-Hispanic Peru." *Geographical Journal,* 1983, Vol. 149, p. 153.

Peterson, I. "Ancient Technology: Pouring A Pyramid." *Science News,* 1984, Vol. 125, p. 327.

Price, Derek de Solla. "Gears from the Greeks." *Transactions of the American Philosophical Society,* (Philadelphia), November 1974.

Protzen, Jean-Pierre. "Inca Stonemasonry." *Scientific American,* February 1986.

"Pyramids Are Not Made of Polymers, Say Experts." *Pursuit,* 1984, Vol. 17, p. 92.

Randi, James. "Atlantean Road: The Bimini Beach-Rock." *The Skeptical Inquirer,* Spring 1981.

Reinhard, Johan. "Sacred Mountains: An Ethno-Archaeological Study of High Andean Ruins." *Mountain Research and Development,* 1985, Vol. 5, no. 4.

Richards, Douglas G. "Archaeological Anoma-lies in the Bahamas." *Journal of Scientific Exploration,* 1988, Vol. 2, no. 2.

Safer, John. "Las Bolas Grandes: An Archaeological Enigma." *Oceans,* July/August 1975.

Salwi, Dilip. "The Enigmatic Pillar of Delhi." *New Scientist,* January 3, 1985.

Schmandt-Besserat, Denise:

"An Archaic Recording System in the Uruk-Jemdet Nasr Period." *American Journal of Archaeology,* 1979, Vol. 83, pp. 19-48.

"The Earliest Precursor of Writing." *Scientific American,* June 1978.

"The Precursor to Numeral and Writing." *Archeology,* November/December 1986.

Sheckley, Robert. "Romans in Rio?" *Omni,* June 1983.

Sherby, O. D., and J. Wadsworth. "Damascus Steels." *Scientific American,* February 1985.

Shinn, E. A. "Atlantis: Bimini Hoax." *Sea Frontiers,* 1978, Vol. 23, pp. 130-141.

Stepston, Harold. "Baalbek the Mysterious." *Scientific American,* 1913, Vol. 109, pp. 456-457.

Stock, Chester. "Origin of the Supposed Human Footprints of Carson City, Nevada." *Science,* 1920, Vol. 51, p. 514.

Sullivan, Walter:

"Artifacts in Rio Bay May Be Roman." *New York Times,* October 10, 1982.

"16th Century Charts Seen as Hinting Ancient Explorers Mapped Antarctica." *New York Times,* September 26, 1984.

Tolstoy, Paul. "Cultural Parallels between Southeast Asia and Mesoamerica in the Manufacture of Bark Cloth." *Transactions of the New York Academy of Sciences,* April 1963.

Topping, Audrey. "China's Incredible Find." *National Geographic,* April 1978.

Wadsworth, J., and O. D. Sherby. "On the Bulat-Damascus Steels Revisited." *Progress in Materials Science,* 1980, Vol. 25, pp. 35-68.

Wesley, W. H. "Footprints of Prehistoric Man." *Knowledge,* 1888, Vol. 12, pp. 28-30.

Other Sources

Barnard, Noel (Ed.). "Oceania and the Americas" (Vol. 3 of *Early Chinese Art and Its Possible Influence in the Pacific Basin).* Symposium. New York: Intercultural Arts Press, 1972.

Capon, Edmund. "Qin Shihuang: Terracotta Warriors and Horses" (3rd ed.). Exhibition catalog. International Cultural Corporation of Australia Limited, 1982.

Carlson, John B., and James Judge (Eds.). *Astronomy and Ceremony in the Prehistoric South.* Papers of the Maxwell Museum of Anthropology, No. 2. Albuquerque: University of New Mexico, 1987.

Erickson, Clark L. "Applied Archaeology and Rural Development: Archaeology's Potential Contribution to the Future." Paper presented at the Circum-Pacific Prehistory Conference, Seattle, Wash., August 2-6, 1989.

Jett, Stephen C. "Further Information on the Geography of the Blowgun, and Its Implications for Early Transoceanic Contacts." Draft paper. Department of Geography, University of California at Davis, no date.

Kendall, Timothy. *Patolli: A Game of Ancient Mexico.* Belmont, Mass.: Kirk Game Co., 1980.

Kjellson, Henry. "Letter to the Editor." *Pursuit,* Third Quarter 1985, Vol. 18, no. 3.

Rowe, John H. "What Kind of Settlement Was Inca Cuzco?" *Nawpa Pacha.* International series for Andean archaeology. Berkeley, Calif.: Institute of Andean Studies, 1967.

PICTURE CREDITS

morial Collection, bequest of Nelson A. Rockefeller—Platin Gilde International Frankfurt, courtesy Museum für Völkerkunde, Staatliche Museen Preussischer Kulturbesitz, West Berlin. **23:** MacQuitty International Photographic Collection, London. **24, 25:** The Metropolitan Museum of Art, bequest of George Cameron Stone, 1936 (36.25.1294a) (2)—cat. no. 311244, photo H. S. Rice, courtesy Department Library Services, American Museum of Natural History, New York. **26, 27:** Jean Vertut—Barry Iverson, courtesy Egyptian Museum, Cairo. **28, 29:** Cloud art by Fred Holz; Barry Iverson, courtesy Egyptian Museum, Cairo; Smithsonian Institution, photo no. 75-6669, Washington, D.C.—line art by Time-Life Books; Larry Sherer, from *Ramayana*, in Ordisi Pata Painting, by Sri Surendra Kumar Das, Panchali Publications, Orissa, India, 1977. **30:** Smithsonian Institution, Department of Anthropology, photo no. 148148, Washington, D.C.—Biblioteca Nacional, Madrid. **31:** MacQuitty International Photographic Collection, London—Scala, Florence. **32:** Musée Gaumais, Virton, Luxembourg—MacQuitty International Photographic Collection, London. **33:** Carmelo Guadagno, courtesy Museum of the American Indian, Heye Foundation, New York (2); cat. no. 326744, courtesy Department Library Services, American Museum of Natural History, New York—Justin Kerr. **34:** The National Museum, Copenhagen, Department of Near Eastern and Classical Antiquities, inventory no. ABb 96. **35:** Craig Aurness/West Light, inset, Massimo Listri/FMR, Milan. **36:** Courtesy San Diego Museum of Man. **38, 39:** From *Seaweeds: A Color-Coded, Illustrated Guide to Common Marine Plants of the East Coast of the United States*, by Charles James Hillson, The Pennsylvania State University, 1977; Massimo Listri/FMR, Milan. **40, 41:** From *The Healing Hand: Man and Wound in the Ancient World*, by Guido Majno, Harvard University Press, 1975—The New York Botanical Garden, photographs and hand coloring by James McInnis. **42:** Courtesy William A. Shear. **43:** Courtesy Biopharm, Ltd.—courtesy Dr. William H. Gotwald, Jr. **44:** The Wellcome Collection, Science Museum, London; Riccardo Villarosa/Overseas s.r.l., Milan, from *Gli Etruschi e il Fegato di Piacenza*, by Viviano Domenici, Camillo Corvi S.P.A., Piacenza, Italy. **45:** Louis Michel Gohel, courtesy Musée de Bar Le-Duc, France. **47:** FPG International, inset, Urs F. Kluyver/Focus, Hamburg, West Germany. **48:** Damm, Düsseldorf/Zefa. **49:** Artwork by Fred Holz. **50:** From *Mazes and Labyrinths: A General Account of Their History and Developments*, by W. H. Matthews, Longmans, Green & Co., London, 1922. **51:** Sonia Halliday, Buckinghamshire, England. **52:** Adam Woolfitt/Woodfin Camp; Nikos Kontos, Athens. **53:**

Hoffman-Buchardi, Düsseldorf/Zefa; Adam Woolfitt/Susan Griggs Agency, London. **54:** Courtesy Thomas and Shelia Pozorski—Urs F. Kluyver/Focus, Hamburg, West Germany. **55:** Robert Frerck/Panoramic Stock Images. **56:** Mark Sherman/Bruce Coleman. **57:** Artwork by Fred Holz—Loren McIntyre (2). **58, 59:** Artwork by Fred Holz. **61:** C. M. Dixon, Kent, England. **62:** Anthony Marshal/Woodfin Camp. **63:** Courtesy Lindley Vann. **64:** Forschungsprojekt Mohenjo-Daro, Aachen Foto Helmes. **65:** Melville Bell Grosvenor, © 1958 National Geographic Society. **66:** Newton Morgan, courtesy William Morgan Architects. **67:** Georg Gerster/Comstock. **68:** Georg Gerster/The John Hillelson Agency, London. **69:** David Brill. **70:** From *The Complete Encylcopedia of Illustration*, by Johann G. Heck, Crown Publishers, New York, 1979. **71:** M. Angelo/West Light, inset, © 1988 Lawrence Migdale/Photo Researchers. **72, 73:** Jean Vertut. **74:** Anna Mitchell-Hedges, F.R.G.S. **75:** Dr. Jevan Berrange/South American Pictures, Suffolk, England. **76:** Courtesy the Trustees of the British Museum, London (2)—Janet and Colin Bord, Wales. **77:** Courtesy Harry Casey. **78, 79:** Courtesy Harry Casey; Malcolm Aird/Robert Estall, Colchester, England; courtesy Marilyn Bridges—courtesy Johan Reinhard; Georg Gerster/Comstock, background Allan Zarling, National Park Service, negative no. 2039. **80:** Courtesy Dr. Suzanne E. Cahill. **81:** Work in Progress/Luisa Ricciarini, Milan—© 1988 Lawrence Migdale/Photo Researchers. **82:** Lino Pellegrini, Milan. **83:** Courtesy Johan Reinhard. **84:** Adam Woolfitt/Susan Griggs Agency, London. **85:** Dennis de Cicco/Sky and Telescope—The Royal Observatory, Edinburgh—Scala, Florence. **86:** Adam Woolfitt/Susan Griggs Agency, London. **87:** Artwork by Fred Holz. **88, 89:** Artwork by Fred Holz, copied by Larry Sherer—artwork by Time-Life Books. **90, 91:** Irving W. Lindelblad, courtesy U.S. Naval Observatory; Bryan and Cherry Alexander, Sturminster, Newton, Dorset, England, from *Masked Dancers of West Africa: The Dogon* (Peoples of the Wild series), © 1982 Time-Life Books; Scala, Florence. **92:** Photograph of disc and details, Scala, Florence—artwork by Fred Holz. **94:** Charalambos Karakalos, Hellenic Atomic Energy Committee, Athens; The National Archaeological Museum, Athens—Cambridge University Library. **95:** John Carlson, Center for Archaeoastronomy, College Park, Maryland—Von Del Chamberlain, Hansen Planetarium, Salt Lake City, Utah. **96:** From *The Complete Encyclopedia of Illustration*, by Johann G. Heck, Crown Publishers, New York, 1979. **97:** Robert Landau/West Light, insets, Landesinstitut für Pädagogik und Medien, Dudweiler, West Germany (2). **98:** Scala, Florence. **99, 100:**

Courtesy the Trustees of the British Museum, London. **101:** Donato Pineider, courtesy Biblioteca Nazionale Centrale, Florence. **102:** Landesinstitut für Pädagogik und Medien, Dudweiler, West Germany. **103:** Erich Lessing, Culture and Fine Arts Archives, Vienna. **104:** Takashi Okamura, Rome—Erich Lessing, Culture and Fine Arts Archives, Vienna. **105:** New Orleans Museum of Art, Women's Volunteer Committee Fund. **106:** Museum of the American Indian, Heye Foundation, New York. **107:** Guy Motil/West Light, inset, Universitätsbibliothek Hiedelberg, West Germany, "Codex Palatinus Germanicus," 60. **108:** Minnesota Historical Society. **109:** From *The Vinland Map and the Tartar Relation*, by R. A. Skelton, T. E. Marston, and G. D. Painter, Yale University Press, 1965. **110:** Dumbarton Oaks Research Library and Collections, Washington, D.C. **111:** Courtesy Carl L. Johannessen. **112:** Courtesy of the Freer Gallery of Art, Smithsonian Institution, Washington, D.C., detail of 14.36 Chinese Stone Sculpture: Eastern Wei (534-550) Buddhist tablet: seated figure of the Buddist Sakymauni in high relief. H: 132.4 x 73.8 cm x depth 38.4 cm; courtesy the Trustees of the British Museum, London. **113:** James H. Pickerell. **114:** Universitätsbibliothek Heidelberg, West Germany, "Codex Palatinus Germanicus," 60. **115:** Nathan Benn/Tim Severin, Brighton, England. **116:** © Janny Kowynia 1989. **117:** Artwork by Time-Life Books. **118, 119:** Artwork by Time-Life Books; Frank Wandell, © 1976 National Geographic Society. **120:** Smithsonian Institution/National Numismatic Collection Photos, Washington, D.C. **121:** Akademische Druck und Verlagsanstalt, Graz, Austria—Larry Sherer, from *Jinshisuo: Illustrated Index to Ancient Bronze and Stone Tablets*, compiled by Yunpeng Feng and Yunyuan Feng, 1820. **122:** Öystein Brochs, courtesy Göteborgs Stad Ethnografiska Museet, Gothenburg, Sweden—Larry Sherer, Smithsonian Natural History Museum, Department of Anthropology, Washington, D.C. **123:** Courtesy Robert F. Marx. **124:** Renee Comet, from *Early Formative Period of Coastal Ecuador: The Valdivia and Machalilla Phases*, by Betty J. Meggers, Clifford Evans, and Emilio Estrada, Smithsonian Institution, Washington, D.C., 1965. **125:** Ken Rogers/West Light, inset, courtesy Ron Calais. **126, 127:** Photo by Ara Güler, Istanbul, courtesy Topkapi Palace Museum, Istanbul, except lower left, map by Fred Holz. **128:** Library of Congress. **130:** Courtesy Ron Calais. **131:** From *The Complete Encyclopedia of Illustration*, by Johann G. Heck, Crown Publishers, New York, 1979; courtesy Glen J. Kuban. **132:** Courtesy Glen J. Kuban. **133:** From *The Complete Encyclopedia of Illustration*, by Johann G. Heck, Crown Publishers, New York, 1979.

INDEX

Cerne Abbas, 80; Great Serpentine Mound of Ohio, 80; Long Man of Wilmington, *78*, 80; Marching Bear Mounds of Iowa, *78-79*, 80; Rock Eagle of Eatonton, Georgia, *79*, 80; Silbury Hill in England, *62*; of Southwest United States, 77, *78-79*, 80. *See also* Stoneworks

Easter Island, *82-83*

Eclipses: ancient prediction of, 85, 89

Ecuador: pre-Columbian mask, *22*; Valdivia excavations, 124

Efem, S. E. E., 39

Eggebrecht, Arne, 20-21

Egypt: electric light in, 26-27; glider model, 19, 28; Great Pyramid of Khufu, 48-50; labyrinth of Amenemhet III, 50; leeching, 42-43; medicinal use of antibacterial molds in, 42; medicinal use of honey in, 38-39; oldest-known brewery in the world, 26; spoons used in ancient times, 12; Suez Canal, 51; Temple of Dendera, *26-27*; topographical maps of, 21

Einstein, Albert, 13

Electric batteries, 20-21

Electric light, 26-27

Electroplating, *20, 21*

Elements of Geometry (Euclid), 10

Elvin-Lewis, Memory, 41

Endocrinology: in ancient China, 35, 38

England: Long Man of Wilmington, *78*, 80; Silbury Hill, *62*; Stonehenge, 47, 60, *61*, 86, 89

Eratosthenes, 10, 87

Eriksson, Leif, 109

Estrada, Emilio, 124

Etruscans: dentistry, *44*; manhunting, *104*

Euclid, 10

Eupalinus, 52

Euripides, *8-9*

F

Farming: ancient Andean techniques, 56-57; reaping machines, 32

Fell, Barry, 117

Fertility: symbols of, 77

Fineus, Orontius, 128-129

Fischer, Steven, 92

Fisherman geoglyph of Arizona, *78*

Flight: pre-history of, 19, 28-30

Flying crafts: tales of in *Ramayana*, 29

Forge welding, 23

Fossils of the South Downs (Mantell), 133

France: Neolithic trepanation of skulls, 36-37

Franklin, Kenneth, 91

G

Galileo, 94

Gambling: among Aztecs, *101*, 106

Games: Aztec ball game, 105; Chinese card playing, 106; go, oldest-known board game, 101; Patolli, board game of Aztecs, 101. *See also* Olympic Games; Sports

Gears, differential: invention of, 94

Gerard, John, 40

Gilgamesh: Sumerian epic poem of, *16*

Gladiators, *97, 102*

Glider: ancient model of, *19, 28*

Gods and goddesses: of the Andes, *54*; Harsomthus, 27; Hathor, 26; Macuilxochitl, 101; Mayuel, 121; Ometochtli, 101; Soma, 121; Thoth, 35

Goiter: treatment for, 38

Goldworking: electroplating technique, 20-21; gilding technique, 22-23

Goodwin, William B., 116

Gordon, Cyrus, 113, 118

Gray, Willard M., 20

Great North Road in Chaco Canyon, 69

Great Pyramid of Khufu, 47, *48-49*, 50

Great Serpentine Mound of Ohio, 80

Great Zimbabwe, *67-68*

Griaule, Marcel, 90

Guanabara Bay, shipwrecks in, 123

H

Hahn, Emma, 130

Halkatha, 28

Hall, Robert, 109

Hammurabi's Code, 46

Hand paintings: of Cro-Magnon man, *73*

Hapgood, Charles H., 128-129; quoted, 127

Harappa, Pakistan, 64

Harvesters. *See* Reaping machines

Heating systems: Roman hypocaust system, 31

Hebrews: ancient tribe in Tennessee, 113

Heinzelin, Jean de, 17

Heliopolis. *See* Baalbek

Hero (Heron) of Alexandria, 10, 19, 28-29

Herodotus, 49, 50

Herophilus of Thrace, 10

Hieroglyphs: on Great Pyramid, 50; of Hammondsville, Ohio, 133; on Mochican lima beans, 13

Hipparchus of Nicea, 10

Hippocrates, 37

Holand, Hjalmar Rued, 109

Holes, Aubrey, 60

Homer, 100

Honey: healing power of, 38-39

Horse harnesses: throat-and-girth, 31; trace, *31*

Human sacrifice, 57, 104

Hydraulus (water organ): invention of, *34*

Hypocaust system, 31

Hypogeum of Malta, *52*

I

I Ching, 11

Incan culture: recordkeeping using *quipu*, 11,

13; walled city of Cuzco, 70

India: Ktub Minar Mosque, 23; medicinal practices, 41, 43; Pillar of Delhi, 23; plastic surgery, 39-40; stone god in temple, *111*

Inoculation: for smallpox, 35, 37

Inventions: aircraft, 19, 28-30; Archimedian screw, 10; battery, 20-21; computer of Antikythera, 94; gears, 94; geological maps, 21; Greek fire weapon, 21; horse harnesses, 31; hypocaust system, 31; light bulbs, 26-27; matches, 27; reaping machines, 32; steam engine, 10, 19, 28-29; threaded screw, 23; water organ, 34; wheel, 33; wheelbarrow, 32

Iodine: medicinal uses of, 38

Ireland: Newgrange, 76, *86-87*

Iron Man of Kottenforst, 25

Ironworking: forgewelding technique, 23; rust-free pillars, 23, 25

J

Japan: Jomon pottery of, 124

Jett, Stephen C., 120

Jívaro Indians: medicinal practices of, 41

Jomon pottery, 124

Jordan: ruins at Petra, *51*

Jupiter, Temple of: in Baalbek, 65

K

Kallipos, 99

The Kensington Rune-Stone Is Genuine (Hall), 109

Kensington stone of Minnesota, *108*, 109

Kepler, Johannes, 10

Knife: early use of, *12*

König, Wilhelm, 20

Ktub Minar Mosque, 23

L

Labyrinth of Amenemhet III, *50*

Labyrinths: design of the ancients, 76-77

Larco Hoyle, Rafael, 13

Lascaux Cave, 72; art detail, *72*

Lavoisier, Antoine, 17

Lebanon: Baalbek, stones of, 65

Leeches: medicinal, 42, 43

Leisky, M., 133

Lewis, David, 119

Lewis, Walter H., 41

Ley, Willy, 20

Light bulbs, 26-27

Lima bean: decorations on pots, 13; hieroglyphics on, 13

Loch Roag in Ireland, 88-89

Long Man of Wilmington, England, *78*, 80

Lubaantan (Mayan city), 73-74

Lucretius, 12

Lukurmata: ruins of, 56

Lunar standstill, *88-89*

M

McCormick, Cyrus, 32
Magellan, Ferdinand, 129
Mahabharata, 29
Mahan, Joseph, 113
Maize, 111
Mallery, Arlington, 127
Malta, Hypogeum of, *52*
Manhunting: of Etruscans, *104*
Mantell, Gideon, 133
Mantracks, *131-132*
Maps: Fineus map of Antarctica, *128*, 129; Lost Map of Columbus, 126; Piri Re'is map of Antarctica, *126*, 127; Turin papyrus map, *21*; Vinland map, *109*, 110
Maps of the Ancient Sea Kings (Hapgood), 127
Marching Bear Mounds of McGregor, Iowa, *78-79*, 80
Marshack, Alexander, 17
Marx, Robert, 123
Masks: pre-Columbian, *22*
Matches: invention of, 27
Mathematics: decimal system, 16; negative numbers, 16; notation, 14; pi, 16; Pythagorean theorem, 18; zero concept, 15
Mauch, Karl, 67-68
Maya: athletic games, 97
Maze. *See* Labyrinths
Medicine: brain surgery, 36-37; cataract surgery, 35, 45-46; couching, 45-46; dental techniques, 44; endocrinology, 35, 38; inoculation, 35, 38; leeching, 42-43; living sutures, 43; organotherapy, 38; plastic surgery, 35, 39, *40*; prosthetic devices, 44; surgical instruments, *36*; trepanation of skulls, 36-37
Megalithic architecture. *See* New Stone Age architecture; Stoneworks
Mental illness: treatment for, 41
Messiha, Khalil, 28
Metalworking: with aluminum, 24, 26; ancient secrets of, 22-23; with Damascus steel, 24-25; electroplating technique, 20-21; forge-welding technique, 23; gilding technique, 23; with platinum, 23; sintering technique, 23. *See also* Goldworking
Meteors, 17
Mikesell, Mike, 129
Millipede: medicinal properties of liquid from, *42*
Milo of Crotona, 100
Minoan culture: bull leaping, *98;* and lost city of Atlantis, 130-131; Phaistos disk, *91-93;* writing, 18
Mirrors: adjustable, invention of, 34; Chinese light penetration, *80*
Mitchell-Hedges, Anna, 74
Mitchell-Hedges, Frederick, 74

Moai (stone heads), *82-83*
Moche culture: metalworking of, 23
Mochica people: irrigation systems, 58; pottery, *7*, *13*; written language of, 13
Mohenjo-Daro in Pakistan, *64*, 65
Monolithic structures. *See* Stoneworks
Monolith of Baalbek, *65*
Moon: Ice age lunar calendars, 17; lunar image of the rabbit, *121*; lunar standstill, 89; size of, 10
Mounds. *See* Earthworks
Mudras, *112*
Mumbahuru (House of the Great Woman), 67
Mummy: corpse of ancient miner, *25;* remains of Incan child, 57
Musical instruments: water organ, *34*
Mystery Hill in New Hampshire, *116-117*

N

Nabatean people, 51
Nan Madol: ruins of, *66*, 67
Nan Zapue: temple of, 66
Navigation: by Greek navigator Pytheas, 117; of Polynesians, 119; by the stars, 121
Nazca Lines of Peru, 77
Negative numbers, 16
Neilsen, Richard, 109
Nero, 99
Neto, Ladislau, 118
Newgrange in Ireland, 76, *86-87*
New Stone Age architecture: Callanish stones, *88-89*; Newgrange, 76, *86-87*; Stonehenge, 86, 89
Newton, Sir Isaac, 88
New World: discovery of, 107; Hebrew settlement in, 113; maize discovery links Old World and, 111; Norse voyages to, 107-109; Phoenician visit to, 118; Roman coins in, 120; Saint Brendan's voyage to, 114-115; Vinland map and, 109-110
Nicaragua: footprints of pre-ancient man, 132
North Star: location of, 117
Nose reconstruction, 39-*40*
Notation. *See* Hieroglyphs; Mathematics, notation; Pictographs; *Quipu* (knotted strings); Writing

O

Oenopides of Chios, 89
Ohman, Olof, 108
O'Kelly, Claire, 86
O'Kelly, Michael, 86
Olmec Indians: ball game of, 105-106
Olympic Games: origins of, 97, 98-100
Orata, Gaius Sergius, 31
Organ (musical instrument): invention of, 34

P

Pachacuti, 70
Pahnkadira, 66-67

Papermaking, 122-123; utensil for beating bark, *122*
Paraiba inscription, 118
Parakramabahu I, *63*
Parsons, James, 133
Patolli (Aztec gambling game), 101
Pattee, Jonathan, 116
Penicillin: early forms of, 42
Pergamon Library (Asia Minor), 9
Pernier, Luigi, 91
Peru: lima-bean hieroglyphics, 13; Nazca Lines, 77; pre-Columbian metalworking, 22-23; pre-Columbian trepanation of skulls, 36-37; *quipu*, 11, 13; stoneworks in Andes, 47
Petra: ruins of, *51*
Petronius, 24
Phaistos Disk, *91-93*
Pharoah's Treasury of Petra, 51
Phoenician visit to New World, 118
Pi, 16
Picasso, Pablo: quoted, 72
Pictographs: on Transylvanian tablets, 18
Pillar of Delhi, 23
Piri Re'is: map of Antarctica, *126*, 127
Planets: elliptical orbit of, 10
Plastic surgery, 35
Platinum, 23
Plato, 130-131
Pliny, 24, 117
Pohnpei, Island of, 66-67
Polybius, 117
Polynesians: early voyages of, *118-119*
Pomerance, Leon, 91-93
Ponce de León, Juan, 115
Pre-ancient civilizations, 125; artifacts of, 132-133; Coso artifact, 129; lost continent of Atlantis, 130-131; maps of ancient seas, 126-128; Texas hammer, 130
Price, Derek de Solla, 93
Prosthetic devices, in the classical era, *44*
Ptolemy I, *8*
Pyramid inch, 48
Pyramids: of Amenemhet III at Fayoum, 50; of the Andes, 54; Great Pyramid of Khufu, 47, 48-50
Pythagoras, 18, 87; family of, 100
Pythagorean theorem, 18
Pytheas, 117

Q

Qin Shi Huangdi: mausoleum of, *71*, *81*, 82
Quinine: for treatment of malaria, 41
Quipu (knotted strings), *11*, 13

R

Rabbit: lunar image of, *121*
Ramayana, 29
Rauwolfia (moonshine plant), *41*
Ray, Tom P., 87

Time-Life Books Inc.
is a wholly owned subsidiary of
THE TIME INC. BOOK COMPANY

President and Chief Executive Officer:
Kelso F. Sutton
President, Time Inc. Books Direct:
Christopher T. Linen

TIME-LIFE BOOKS INC.

EDITOR: George Constable
Executive Editor: Ellen Phillips
Director of Design: Louis Klein
Director of Editorial Resources: Phyllis K. Wise
Director of Photography and Research:
John Conrad Weiser

PRESIDENT: John M. Fahey, Jr.
Senior Vice Presidents: Robert M. DeSena,
Paul R. Stewart, Curtis G. Viebranz, Joseph J. Ward
Vice Presidents: Stephen L. Bair, Bonita L.
Boezeman, Mary P. Donohoe, Stephen L. Goldstein,
Juanita T. James, Andrew P. Kaplan, Trevor Lunn,
Susan J. Maruyama, Robert H. Smith
New Product Development: Yuri Okuda,
Donia Ann Steele
Supervisor of Quality Control: James King

PUBLISHER: Joseph J. Ward

Editorial Operations
Copy Chief: Diane Ullius
Production: Celia Beattie
Library: Louise D. Forstall
Computer Composition: Gordon E. Buck
(Manager), Deborah G. Tait, Monika D. Thayer,
Janet Barnes Syring, Lillian Daniels

**Library of Congress
Cataloging-in-Publication Data**
Feats and wisdom of the ancients / by the editors of
Time-Life Books.
p.   cm.   (Library of curious and unusual facts).
Bibliography: p.
Includes index.
ISBN 0-8094-7675-4
ISBN 0-8094-7676-2 (lib. bdg.)
1.Civilization, Ancient—Miscellanea.
2.Curiosities and wonders.
I.Time-Life Books. II. Series.
CB311.F43 1990
930   89-20519 CIP

LIBRARY OF CURIOUS AND UNUSUAL FACTS

SERIES DIRECTOR: Russell B. Adams, Jr.
Series Administrator: Elise Ritter Gibson
Designer: Susan K. White
Associate Editors: Sally Collins,
Blaine Marshall (pictures)

Editorial Staff for
Feats and Wisdom of the Ancients
Text Editors: Laura Foreman (principal),
Carl A. Posey
Researchers: Susan Stuck (principal),
Sydney J. Baily, Roxie France-Nuriddin,
Charlotte Fullerton, M. Tucker Jones,
Robert H. Wooldridge, Jr.
Assistant Designer: Alan Pitts
Copy Coordinators: Jarelle S. Stein (principal),
Darcie Conner Johnston
Picture Coordinator: Kate Griffin
Editorial Assistant: Terry Ann Paredes

Special Contributors: Lesley Coleman, Christine
Hinze (London research); William Barnhill, Sarah
Brash, Dan Darvishian, Donal Gordon, Sandra
Salmans, John Sullivan, Ricardo Villanueva, Roger
Witherspoon (text); Bill Battaile, Jr., Kathryn Pfeifer
(research); Victoria Agee (index)

Correspondents: Elisabeth Kraemer-Singh (Bonn),
Christina Lieberman (New York), Maria Vincenza
Aloisi (Paris), Ann Natanson (Rome).
Valuable assistance was also provided by Wibo Van
de Linde (Amsterdam); Mirka Gondicas (Athens);
Brigid Grauman, (Brussels); Nihal Tamraz (Cairo);
Barbara Gevene Hertz (Copenhagen); Ara Güler
(Istanbul); Elizabeth Brown (New York); Dag Chris-
tensen (Oslo); Ann Wise (Rome); Mary Johnson
(Stockholm); Dick Berry, Mieko Ikeda (Tokyo);
Traudl Lessing (Vienna).

The Consultants:
William R. Corliss, the general consultant for the
series, is a physicist-turned-writer who has spent the
last twenty-five years compiling collections of
anomalies in the fields of geophysics, geology, archaeology, astronomy, biology, and psychology. He
has written about science and technology for NASA,
the National Science Foundation, and the Energy
Research and Development Administration (among
others). Mr. Corliss is also the author of more than
thirty books on scientific mysteries, including *Mysterious Universe, The Unfathomed Mind,* and *Handbook of Unusual Natural Phenomena.*

John B. Carlson helped develop a new interdiscipli-
nary specialty, the study of astronomy in ancient
cultures. He is founder and director of the Center
for Archaeoastronomy, in College Park, Maryland.

Kenneth L. Feder, associate professor in anthropology at Central Connecticut State University, is a con-
sulting editor for *The Skeptical Inquirer.*

Bob Rickard is the founder and editor of *The
Fortean Times* in London and coauthor of *Phenomena: A Book of Wonders.* To preserve rare data and
documentation he has also founded the Fortean
archives and picture library.

John Scarborough is professor of the history of
pharmacy and medicine at the University of Wisconsin. He has published extensively on Greek, Roman,
and Byzantine pharmacy, zoology, and botany.

Marcello Truzzi, a professor of sociology at Eastern
Michigan University, is also director of the Center
for Scientific Anomalies Research (CSAR) and editor
of its journal, *Zetetic Scholar.*

Stephen Williams is Peabody Professor of American
archaeology and ethnology at Harvard University and
also serves as curator of North American archaeology at the Peabody Museum.

Other Publications: